Ezra Abbot, Andrew Preston Peabody

The fourth Gospel

Evidence external and internal of its Johannean authorship

Ezra Abbot, Andrew Preston Peabody

The fourth Gospel
Evidence external and internal of its Johannean authorship

ISBN/EAN: 9783337281496

Printed in Europe, USA, Canada, Australia, Japan

Cover: Foto ©Thomas Meinert / pixelio.de

More available books at **www.hansebooks.com**

THE FOURTH GOSPEL

EVIDENCES EXTERNAL AND INTERNAL OF ITS
JOHANNEAN AUTHORSHIP

BY

EZRA ABBOT, D.D.

ANDREW P. PEABODY, D.D.

AND

J. B. LIGHTFOOT, D.D.

Bishop of Durham

London

HODDER AND STOUGHTON

27, PATERNOSTER ROW

MDCCCXCII

CONTENTS.

PREFACE.

Of the first of these Essays it can hardly be necessary to say anything which is not included in the author's name. In his special department Dr. Abbot was recognized, on both sides of the Atlantic, as second to no scholar of his time. He was indefatigably painstaking and exhaustively thorough in his researches, and there never went from his hands any but finished work. He had his own dearly cherished religious beliefs; but they were always held as subject to revision on adequate evidence. His impartiality in investigation, and his willingness to yield preconceived opinions on adequate ground, add great weight to his firm conviction of the Johannean authorship of the Fourth Gospel.

Dr. Abbot's expression of disappointment that he had not been able to write on the internal tokens of authorship in the Fourth Gospel directed my special attention to the subject. In treating it, I determined to consult no authority except the Gospel itself; and my Essay is the result of a close and careful study of the Gospel. This study has so far modified my opinion that, while I previously believed that John wrote that Gospel, I now feel sure that no one but John could have written it.

Bishop Lightfoot's paper was a lecture in a course on the Evidences of Christianity, delivered at St. George's Hall, in Liverpool, in 1871. He prepared it for publication in *The Expositor* shortly before his death, and it appeared in the numbers of that periodical for January, February, and March, 1890. In itself of inestimable value, its worth is even enhanced by the fact that after an interval of eighteen years he found "nothing to withdraw." In that interval he had lectured on the Fourth Gospel in Cambridge, and had been constantly engaged in studies appertaining to the history and authority of the canon of the New Testament. No man can have kept himself more entirely on a level with the foremost scholarship of the time than he, nor was he exceeded by any of his contemporaries in his uniformly fair and candid treatment of those who occupied a different ground from his own. That on the points at issue his opinions suffered no change is a pledge of their soundness.

ANDREW P. PEABODY.

I.

THE AUTHORSHIP OF THE FOURTH GOSPEL: EXTERNAL EVIDENCE.

By Ezra Abbot.

PREFATORY NOTE TO THE FIRST ESSAY.

THE following essay was read, in part, before the "Ministers' Institute," at its public meeting last October, in Providence, R.I. In considering the external evidences of the genuineness of the Gospel ascribed to John, it was out of the question, under the circumstances, to undertake anything more than the discussion of a few important points; and even these could not be properly treated within the time allowed.

In revising the paper for the *Unitarian Review* (February, March, June, 1880), and, with additions and corrections, for the volume of "Institute Essays," I have greatly enlarged some parts of it, particularly that relating to the evidence that the Fourth Gospel was used by Justin Martyr. The consideration of his quotations and of the hypotheses connected with them has given occasion to the long Notes appended to the essay, in which will be found the results of some original investigation. But the circumstances under which the essay is printed have compelled me to treat other parts of the evidence for the genuineness of this Gospel less thoroughly than I wished, and on certain points to content myself with mere references. It has also been necessary to give in a translation many quotations which scholars would have preferred to see in the original; but the translation has been made as literal as the English idiom would permit, and precise references to the passages cited are always given for the benefit of the critical student.

E. A.

CAMBRIDGE, MASS., May 21, 1880.

I.

THE AUTHORSHIP OF THE FOURTH GOSPEL: EXTERNAL EVIDENCES.

The problem of the Fourth Gospel — that is, the question of its authorship and historical value — requires for its complete solution a consideration of many collateral questions which are still in debate. Until these are gradually disposed of by thorough investigation and discussion, we can hardly hope for a general agreement on the main question at issue. Such an agreement among scholars certainly does not at present exist. Since the "epoch-making" essay (to borrow a favorite phrase of the Germans) of Ferdinand Christian Baur, in the *Theologische Jahrbücher* for 1844, there has indeed been much shifting of ground on the part of the opponents of the genuineness of the Gospel; but among scholars of equal learning and ability, as Hilgenfeld, Keim, Scholten, Hausrath, Renan, on the one hand, and Godet, Beyschlag, Luthardt, Weiss, Lightfoot, on the other, opinions are yet divided, with a tendency, at least in Germany, toward the denial of its genuineness. Still, some of these collateral questions of which I have spoken seem to be approaching a settlement. I may notice first one of the most important, the question whether the relation of the Apostle John to Jewish Christianity was not such that it is impossible to suppose the Fourth Gospel to have proceeded from him, even at a late period of his life. This is a fundamental postulate of the theory of the Tübingen School, in regard to the opposition of Paul to the three great Apostles, Peter, James, and John. The Apostle John, they say, wrote the Apocalypse, the most Jewish of all the books of the New Testament; but he could not have written the anti-Judaic Gospel. Recognizing most fully the great service which Baur and his followers have rendered to the history of primitive Christianity by their bold and searching investigations, I think it may be said that there is a wide-spread and deepening conviction among fair-minded scholars that the theory of the Tübingen School, in the form in which it has been presented by the coryphæi of the party, as Baur, Schwegler, Zeller, is an extreme view, resting largely on a false interpretation of many passages of the New Testament, and a false view of many early Christian writings. Matthew Arnold's protest against the excessive "vigour and rigour" of the Tübingen theories brings a good deal of plain English common-sense to bear on the subject, and exposes well some of the extravagances of Baur and others.* Still more weight is to be attached to the emphatic dissent of such an able and thoroughly independent scholar as Dr. James Donaldson, the author of the *Critical History of Christian Literature and Doctrine*, a work unhappily unfinished. But very significant is the remarkable article of Keim on the Apostolic Council at Jerusalem, in his latest work, *Aus dem Urchristenthum* ("Studies in the History of Early Christianity"), published in 1878, a short time before his lamented death. In this able essay, he demolishes the foundation of the Tübingen theory, vindicating in the main the historical character of the account in the Acts, and exposing the misinterpretation of the passage in the Epistle to the Galatians, on which Baur and his followers found their view of the absolute contradiction between the Acts and the Epistle. Holtzmann, Lipsius, Pfleiderer, and especially Weizsäcker had already gone far in modifying the extreme view of Baur; but this essay of Keim's is a re-examination of the whole question with reference to all the recent discussions. The still later work of Schenkel,

---

* See his *God and the Bible*, Preface, and chaps. v . vi.

published during the present year (1879), *Das Christusbild der Apostel und der nachapostolischen Zeit* ("The Picture of Christ presented by the Apostles and by the Post-Apostolic Time"), is another conspicuous example of the same reaction. Schenkel remarks in the Preface to this volume: —

Having never been able to convince myself of the sheer opposition between Petrinism and Paulinism, it has also never been possible for me to get a credible conception of a reconciliation effected by means of a literature sailing between the contending parties under false colors. In respect to the Acts of the Apostles, in particular, I have been led in part to different results from those represented by the modern critical school. I have been forced to the conviction that it is a far more trustworthy source of information than is commonly allowed on the part of the modern criticism; that older documents worthy of credit, besides the well-known *We*-source, are contained in it; and that the Paulinist who composed it has not intentionally distorted (*entstellt*) the facts, but only placed them in the light in which they appeared to him and must have appeared to him from the time and circumstances under which he wrote. He has not, in my opinion, artificially brought upon the stage either a Paulinized Peter, or a Petrinized Paul, in order to mislead his readers, but has portrayed the two apostles just as he actually conceived of them on the basis of his incomplete information. (Preface, pp. x., xi.)

It would be hard to find two writers more thoroughly independent, whatever else may be said of them, than Keim and Schenkel. Considering their well-known position, they will hardly be stigmatized as "apologists" in the contemptuous sense in which that term is used by some recent writers, who seem to imagine that they display their freedom from partisan bias by giving their opponents bad names. On this subject of the one-sidedness of the Tübingen School, I might also refer to the very valuable remarks of Professor Fisher in his recent work on *The Beginnings of Christianity*, and in his earlier volume on *The Supernatural Origin of Christianity*. One of the ablest discussions of the question will also be found in the Essay on "St. Paul and the Three," appended to the commentary on the Epistle to the Galatians, by Professor Lightfoot, now Bishop of Durham, a scholar who has no superior among the Germans in breadth of learning and thoroughness of research. The dissertation of Professor

Jowett on "St. Paul and the Twelve," though not very definite in its conclusions, likewise deserves perusal.*

In regard to this collateral question, then, I conceive that decided progress has been made in a direction favorable to the possibility (to put it mildly) of the Johannean authorship of the Fourth Gospel. We do not know anything concerning the theological position of the Apostle John, which justifies us in assuming that twenty years after the destruction of Jerusalem he could not have written such a work.

Another of these collateral questions, on which a vast amount has been written, and on which very confident and very untenable assertions have been made, may now, I believe, be regarded as set at rest, so far as concerns our present subject, the authorship of the Fourth Gospel. I refer to the history of the Paschal controversies of the second century. The thorough discussion of this subject by Schürer, formerly Professor Extraordinarius at Leipzig, and now Professor at Giessen, the editor of the *Theologische Literaturzeitung*, and author of the excellent *Neutestamentliche Zeitgeschichte*, has clearly shown, I believe, that no argument against the Johannean authorship of the Fourth Gospel can be drawn from the entangled history of these controversies. His essay, in which the whole previous literature of the subject is carefully reviewed, and all the original sources critically examined, was published in Latin at Leipzig in 1869 under the title *De Controversiis Paschalibus secundo post Christum natum Saeculo exortis*, and afterwards in a German translation in Kahnis's *Zeitschrift für die historische Theologie* for 1870, pp. 182–284. There is, according to him, absolutely *no* evidence that the Apostle John celebrated Easter with the Quartodecimans on the 14th of Nisan in commemoration, as is so often assumed, of the day of the *Lord's Supper*. The choice of the day had no reference

* In his work on *The Epistles of St. Paul to the Thessalonians, Galatians, Romans*, 2d ed. (London, 1859), i. 417–477; reprinted in a less complete form from the first edition in Noyes's *Theol. Essays* (1856), p. 357 ff. The very judicious remarks of Mr. Norton in the *Christian Examiner* for May, 1829, vol. vi. p. 200 ff., are still worth reading. See the valuable article of Dr. Wilibald Grimm, "Der Apostelconvent," in the *Stud. u. Krit.*, 1880, pp. 405–432; also, Dr. H. H. Wendt's *Neubearbeitung* of Meyer's *Kommentar* on the Acts, 5e Aufl., Göttingen, 1880. See also Reuss, *Hist. apostolique* (1876), and *Les Epîtres pauliniennes* (1878), in his *La Bible, trad. nouvelle*, etc. Contra, Hilgenfeld, *Zeitschr.*, 1879, p. 100 ff; 1880, p. 1 ff.

to that event, nor on the other hand, as Weitzel and Steitz maintain, to the supposed day of Christ's death, but was determined by the fact that the 14th was the day of the Jewish Passover, for which the Christian festival was substituted. The celebration was Christian, but the *day* adopted by John and the Christians of Asia Minor generally was the *day* of the Jewish Passover, the 14th of Nisan, on whatever day of the week it might fall, while the Western Christians generally, without regard to the day of the month, celebrated Easter on Sunday, in commemoration of the day of the resurrection. This is the view essentially of Lücke, Gieseler, Bleek, De Wette, Hase, and Riggenbach, with differences on subordinate points; but Schürer has made the case clearer than any other writer. Schürer is remarkable among German scholars for a calm, judicial spirit, and for thoroughness of investigation; and his judgment in this matter is the more worthy of regard, as he does not receive the Gospel of John as genuine. A good exposition of the subject, founded on Schürer's discussion, may be found in Luthardt's work on the *Authorship of the Fourth Gospel*, of which an English translation has been published, with an Appendix by Dr. Gregory of Leipzig, giving the literature of the whole controversy on the authorship of the Gospel far more completely than it has ever before been presented.

Another point may be mentioned, as to which there has come to be a general agreement; namely, that the very late date assigned to the Gospel by Baur and Schwegler, namely, somewhere between the years 160 and 170 A.D., cannot be maintained. Zeller and Scholten retreat to 150; Hilgenfeld, who is at last constrained to admit its use by Justin Martyr, goes back to between 130 and 140; Renan now says 125 or 130; Keim in the first volume of his *History of Jesus of Nazara* placed it with great confidence between the years 110 and 115, or more loosely, A.D. 100–117.* The fatal consequences of such an admission as that were, however, soon perceived; and in the last volume of his *History*

* *Geschichte Jesu von Nazara*, i. 155, comp. 146 (Eng. trans. i. 211, comp. 199).

of Jesus, and in the last edition of his abridgment of that work, he goes back to the year 130.* Schenkel assigns it to A.D. 115–120.†

This enforced shifting of the date of the Gospel to the earlier part of the second century (which I may remark incidentally is fatal to the theory that its author borrowed from Justin Martyr instead of Justin from John) at once presents very serious difficulties on the supposition of the spuriousness of the Gospel. It is the uniform tradition, supported by great weight of testimony, that the Evangelist John lived to a very advanced age, spending the latter portion of his life in Asia Minor, and dying there in the reign of Trajan, not far from A.D. 100. How could a spurious Gospel of a character so peculiar, so different from the earlier Synoptic Gospels, so utterly unhistorical as it is affirmed to be, gain currency as the work of the Apostle both among Christians and the Gnostic heretics, if it originated only twenty-five or thirty years after his death, when so many who must have known whether he wrote such a work or not were still living?

The feeling of this difficulty seems to have revived the theory, put forward, to be sure, as long ago as 1840 by a very wild German writer, Lützelberger, but which Baur and Strauss deemed unworthy of notice, that the Apostle John was never in Asia Minor at all. This view has recently found strenuous advocates in Keim, Scholten, and others, though it is rejected and, I believe, fully refuted by critics of the same school, as Hilgenfeld. The historical evidence against it seems to me decisive; and to attempt to support it, as Scholten does, by purely arbitrary conjectures, such as the denial of the genuineness of the letter of Irenæus to Florinus, can only give one the impression that the writer has a desperate cause.‡

---

* *Geschichte Jesu . . . für weitere Kreise*, 3e Bearbeitung, 2e Aufl. (1875), p. 40.

† *Das Charakterbild Jesu*, 4e Aufl. (1873), p. 370.

‡ See Hilgenfeld, *Hist. Krit. Einleitung in d. N. T.* (1875), p. 394 ff.; Bleek, *Einl. in d. N. T.*, 3e Aufl. (1875), p. 167 ff., with Mangold's note; Fisher, *The Beginnings of Christianity* (1877), p. 327 ff. Compare Renan, *L'Antechrist*, p. 557 ff.

Thus far we have noticed a few points connected with the controversy about the authorship of the Fourth Gospel in respect to which some progress may seem to have been made since the time of Baur. Others will be remarked upon incidentally, as we proceed. But to survey the whole field of discussion in an hour's discourse is impossible. To treat the question of the historical evidence with any thoroughness would require a volume; to discuss the internal character of the Gospel in its bearings on the question of its genuineness and historical value would require a much larger one. All therefore which I shall now attempt will be to consider some points of the historical evidence for the genuineness of the Fourth Gospel, as follows:—

1. The general reception of the Four Gospels as genuine among Christians in the last quarter of the second century.

2. The inclusion of the Fourth Gospel in the Apostolical Memoirs of Christ appealed to by Justin Martyr.

3. Its use by the various Gnostic sects.

4. The attestation appended to the book itself.

I. I BEGIN with the statement, which cannot be questioned, that our present four Gospels, and no others, were received by the great body of Christians as genuine and sacred books during the last quarter of the second century. This appears most clearly from the writings of Irenæus, born not far from A.D. 125–130,* whose youth was spent in Asia Minor, and who became Bishop of Lyons in Gaul, A.D. 178; of Clement, the head of the Catechetical School at Alexandria about the year 190, who had travelled in Greece, Italy, Syria, and Palestine, seeking religious instruction; and of Tertullian, in North Africa, who flourished toward the close of the century. The four Gospels are found in the ancient Syriac version of the New Testament, the Peshito, made in the second century, the authority of which has the more weight as it omits the Second and Third Epistles of John, Second Peter, Jude, and the Apocalypse, books whose authorship was disputed in the early Church. Their existence in the Old Latin version also

* About A.D. 115, according to Zahn in Herzog, 2d ed., vii. 135 sq.; see Smith and Wace's *Dict. of Christ. Biogr.* iii. 253.

attests their currency in North Africa, where that version originated some time in the second century. They appear, moreover, in the Muratorian Canon, written probably about A.D. 170, the oldest list of canonical books which has come down to us.

Mr. Norton in his work on the *Genuineness of the Gospels* argues with great force that, when we take into consideration the peculiar character of the Gospels, and the character and circumstances of the community by which they were received, the fact of their universal reception at this period admits of no reasonable explanation except on the supposition that they are genuine. I do not here contend for so broad an inference: I only maintain that this fact proves that our four Gospels could not have originated at this period, but must have been in existence long before; and that some very powerful influence must have been at work to effect their universal reception. I shall not recapitulate Mr. Norton's arguments; but I would call attention to one point on which he justly lays great stress, though it is often overlooked; namely, that the main evidence for the genuineness of the Gospels is of an altogether different kind from that which can be adduced for the genuineness of any classical work. It is not the testimony of a few eminent Christian writers to their private opinion, but it is the evidence which they afford of the belief of the whole body of Christians; and this, not in respect to ordinary books, whose titles they might easily take on trust, but respecting books in which they were most deeply interested; books which were the very foundation of that faith which separated them from the world around them, exposed them to hatred, scorn, and persecution, and often demanded the sacrifice of life itself.

I would add that the greater the differences between the Gospels, real or apparent, the more difficult it must have been for them to gain this universal reception, except on the supposition that they had been handed down from the beginning as genuine. This remark applies particularly to the Fourth Gospel when compared with the first three.

The remains of Christian literature in the first three quarters of the second century are scanty, and are of such a character that, assuming the genuineness of the Gospels, we have really no reason to expect more definite references to their writers, and more numerous quotations from or allusions to them than we actually do find or seem to find. A few letters, as the Epistle of Clement of Rome to the Corinthians, now made complete by the discovery of a new MS. and of a Syriac version of it; the Epistle ascribed to Barnabas, now complete in the original; the short Epistle of Polycarp to the Philippians, and the Epistles (of very doubtful genuineness) attributed to Ignatius; an allegorical work, *the Shepherd* of Hermas, which nowhere quotes either the Old Testament or the New; a curious romance, the *Clementine Homilies;* and the writings of the Christian Apologists, Justin Martyr, Tatian, Theophilus, Athenagoras, Hermias, who, in addressing heathens, could not be expected to talk about Matthew, Mark, Luke, and John, which would be to them names without significance,—these few documents constitute nearly all the literature of the period. As we should not expect the Gospels to be quoted by name in the writings of the Apologists, though we do find John expressly mentioned by Theophilus, so in such a discussion as that of Justin Martyr with Trypho the Jew, Justin could not cite in direct proof of his doctrines works the authority of which the Jew would not recognize, though he might use them, as he does, in attestation of historic facts which he regarded as fulfilling prophecies of the Old Testament.

The author of *Supernatural Religion,* in discussing the evidence of the use of our present Gospels in the first three quarters of the second century, proceeds on two assumptions: one, that in the first half of this century vast numbers of spurious Gospels and other writings bearing the names of Apostles and their followers were in circulation in the early Church; and the other, that we have a right to expect great accuracy of quotation from the Christian Fathers, especially when they introduce the words of Christ with such a formula as "he said" or "he taught." Now this last assumption admits of being thoroughly tested, and it contradicts the most unquestionable facts. Instead of such accuracy of quotation as is assumed as the basis of his argument, it is beyond all dispute that the Fathers often quote very loosely, from memory, abridging, transposing, paraphrasing, amplifying, substituting synonymous words or equivalent expressions, combining different passages together, and occasionally mingling their own inferences with their citations. In regard to the first assumption, a careful sifting of the evidence will show, I believe, that there is really no *proof* that in the time of Justin Martyr (with the possible exception of the Gospel according to the Hebrews, which in its primitive form may have been the Hebrew original from which our present Greek Gospel ascribed to Matthew was mainly derived) there was a single work, bearing the title of a Gospel, which as a *history of Christ's ministry* came into competition with our present four Gospels, or which took the place among Christians which our Gospels certainly held in the last quarter of the second century. Much confusion has arisen from the fact that the term "Gospel" was in ancient times applied to speculative works which gave the writer's view of the Gospel, *i.e.*, of the doctrine of Christ, or among the Gnostics, which set forth their *gnosis*; *e.g.*, among the followers of Basilides, Hippolytus tells us, "the Gospel" is [illegible] "the knowledge of supermundane things" (*Ref. Hær.* vii. 27). Again, the apocryphal Gospels of the Nativity and the Infancy, or such works as the so-called Gospel of Nicodemus, describing the descent of Christ into Hades, have given popular currency to the idea that there were floating about in the middle of the second century a great number of Gospels, rival histories of Christ's ministry; which these apocryphal Gospels, however, are not and do not pretend to be. Other sources of confusion, as the blunders of writers like Epiphanius, I pass over. To enter into a discussion and elucidation of this subject here is of course impossible: I will only recommend the reading of Mr. Norton's full examination of it in the third volume of his *Genuineness of the Gospels*, which needs, to be sure, a little supplementing, but the main positions of which I believe to be impregnable.

Resting on these untenable assumptions, the author of *Supernatural Religion* subjects this early fragmentary literature to a minute examination, and explains away what seem to be quotations from or references to our present Gospels in these different works as borrowed from some of the multitudinous Gospels which he assumes to have been current among the early Christians, especially if these quotations and references do not present a perfect verbal correspondence with our present Gospels, as is the case with the great majority of them. Even if the correspondence is verbally exact, this proves nothing, in his view; for the quotations of the words of Jesus might be borrowed from other current Gospels which resembled ours as much as Matthew, Mark, and Luke resemble each other. But, if the verbal agreement is *not* exact, we have in his judgment a strong proof that the quotations are derived from some apocryphal book. So he comes to the conclusion that there is no certain trace of the existence of our present Gospels for about one hundred and fifty years after the death of Christ; *i.e.*, we will say, till about A.D. 180.

But here a question naturally arises: How is it, if no trace of their existence is previously discoverable, that our four Gospels are suddenly found toward the end of the second century to be received as sacred books throughout the whole Christian world? His reply is, "It is totally unnecessary for me to account for this."* He stops his investigation of the subject just at the point where we have solid facts, not conjectures, to build upon. When he comes out of the twilight into the full blaze of day, he shuts his eyes, and refuses to see anything. Such a procedure cannot be satisfactory to a sincere inquirer after the truth. The fallacy of this mode of reasoning is so well illustrated by Mr. Norton, that I must quote a few sentences. He says:—

> About the end of the second century the Gospels were reverenced as sacred books by a community dispersed over the world, composed of men of different nations and languages. There were, to say the least, sixty thousand copies of them in existence;† they were read in the

* *Supernatural Religion*, 6th edition (18[illegible]), and 7th edition (1879), vol. i. p. ix. (Preface.)

† See Norton's *Genuineness of the Gospels*, 2d ed., i. 45-54.

churches of Christians; they were continually quoted, and appealed to, as of the highest authority; their reputation was as well established among believers from one end of the Christian community to the other, as it is at the present day among Christians in any country. But it is asserted that before that period we find no trace of their existence; and it is, therefore, inferred that they were not in common use, and but little known, even if extant in their present form. This reasoning is of the same kind as if one were to say that the first mention of Egyptian Thebes is in the time of Homer. He, indeed, describes it as a city which poured a hundred armies from its hundred gates; but his is the first mention of it, and therefore we have no reason to suppose that, before his time, it was a place of any considerable note.*

As regards the general reception of the four Gospels in the last quarter of the second century, however, a slight qualification is to be made. Some time in the latter half of the second century, the genuineness of the Gospel of John was denied by a few eccentric individuals (we have no ground for supposing that they formed a sect), whom Epiphanius (*Hær.* li., comp. liv.) calls *Alogi* (Ἄλογοι), a nickname which has the double meaning of "deniers of the doctrine of the Logos," and "men without reason." They are probably the same persons as those of whom Irenæus speaks in one passage (*Hær.* iii. 11. § 9), but to whom he gives no name. But the fact that their difficulty with the Gospel was a doctrinal one, and that they appealed to no tradition in favor of their view; that they denied the Johannean authorship of the Apocalypse likewise, and absurdly ascribed both books to Cerinthus, who, unless all our information about him is false, could not possibly have written the Fourth Gospel, shows that they were persons of no critical judgment. Zeller admits (*Theol. Jahrb.* 1845, p. 645) that their opposition does not prove that the Gospel was not generally regarded in their time as of Apostolic origin. The fact that they ascribed the Fourth Gospel to Cerinthus, a heretic of the first century, contemporary with the Apostle John, shows that they could not pretend that this Gospel was a recent work.

Further, while the Gnostics generally agreed with the

* *Evidences of the Genuineness of the Gospels*, second edition, vol. i. pp. 195, 196

Catholic Christians in receiving the four Gospels, and especially the Gospel of John, which the Valentinians, as Irenæus tells us, used *plenissime* (*Hær.* iii. 11. § 7), the Marcionites are an exception. They did not, however, question the genuineness of the Gospels, but regarded their authors as under the influence of Jewish prejudices. Marcion therefore rejected all but Luke, the Pauline Gospel, and cut out from this whatever he deemed objectionable. We may note here, incidentally, that the author of *Supernatural Religion*, in the first six editions of his work, contended, in opposition to the strongest evidence, that Marcion's Gospel, instead of being, as all ancient testimony represents it, a mutilated Luke, was the earlier, original Gospel, of which Luke's was a later amplification. This theory was started by Semler, that *varium, mutabile et mirabile capitulum*, as he is called by a German writer (Matthæi, *N.T. Gr.*, i. 687); and after having been adopted by Eichhorn and many German critics was so thoroughly refuted by Hilgenfeld in 1850, and especially by Volkmar in 1852, that it was abandoned by the most eminent of its former supporters, as Ritschl, Zeller, and partially by Baur. But individuals differ widely in their power of resisting evidence opposed to their prejudices, and the author of *Supernatural Religion* has few equals in this capacity. We may therefore feel that something in these interminable discussions is settled, when we note the fact that *he* has at last surrendered. His conversion is due to Dr. Sanday, who in an article in the *Fortnightly Review* (June, 1875, p. 855, ff.), reproduced in substance in his work on *The Gospels in the Second Century*, introduced the linguistic argument, showing that the very numerous and remarkable peculiarities of language and style which characterize the parts of Luke which Marcion retained are found so fully and completely in those which he rejected as to render diversity of authorship utterly incredible.

But to return to our first point,—the unquestioned reception of our present Gospels throughout the Christian world in the last quarter of the second century, and that, I add, without the least trace of any previous controversy on the subject, with the insignificant exception of the Alogi whom I have mentioned. This fact has a most important bearing on the next question in order; namely, whether the Apostolical Memoirs to which Justin Martyr appeals about the middle of the second century were or were not our four Gospels. To discuss this question fully would require a volume. All that I propose now is to place the subject in the light of acknowledged facts, and to illustrate the falsity of the premises from which the author of *Supernatural Religion* reasons.

II. The writings of Justin consist of two Apologies or Defences of Christians and Christianity addressed to the Roman Emperor and Senate, the first written most probably about the year 146 or 147 (though many place it in the year 138),* and a Dialogue in defence of Christianity with Trypho the Jew, written somewhat later (*Dial.* c. 120, comp. *Apol.* i. c. 26).†

In these writings, addressed, it is to be observed, to unbelievers, he quotes, not in proof of doctrines, but as authority for his account of the teaching of Christ and the facts in his life, certain works of which he commonly speaks as the "Memoirs" or "Memorabilia" of Christ, using the Greek word, Ἀπομνημονεύματα, with which we are familiar as the designation of the Memorabilia of Socrates by Xenophon. Of these books he commonly speaks as the "Memoirs by the Apostles," using this expression eight times; ‡ four times he calls them "the Memoirs" simply; || once, "Memoirs made by the Apostles which are called Gospels" (*Apol.* i. 66); once, when he cites a passage apparently from the Gospel of Luke, "Memoirs composed by the Apostles of Christ and their companions,"—literally, "those who followed with them" (*Dial.* c. 103); once again (*Dial.* c. 106), when he speaks of our Saviour as changing the name of Peter, and of his giving to James and John the name Boanerges, a fact only mentioned

* So Waddington, *Mém. de l'Acad. des inscr. et belles-lettres*, t. xxvi., pt. i., p. 264 ff.; Harnack in *Theol. Literaturzeitung*, 1876, col. 14, and Caspari, as there referred to; [Lightfoot, *Apostolic Fathers*, pt. ii., vol. i. p. 462].

† See Engelhardt, *Das Christenthum Justins des Märtyrers* (1878), p. 71 ff.; Renan, *L'Eglise chrétienne* (1879), p. 367, n. 4.

‡ *Apol.* i. 67; *Dial.* cc. 100, 101, 102, 103, 104, 106 *bis*: τὰ ἀπομνημονεύματα τῶν ἀποστόλων (τῶν ἀποστ. αὐτοῦ, sc. Χριστοῦ, 5 times).

|| *Dial.* cc. 105 *ter*, 107.

so far as we know in the Gospel of Mark, he designates as his authority "Peter's Memoirs," which, supposing him to have used our Gospels, is readily explained by the fact that Peter was regarded by the ancients as furnishing the materials for the Gospel of Mark, his travelling companion and interpreter.* Once more, Justin speaks in the plural of "those who have written Memoirs (οἱ ἀπομνημονεύσαντες) of all things concerning our Saviour Jesus Christ, whom (οἷς) we believe" (*Apol.* i. 33); and, again, "the Apostles wrote" so and so, referring to an incident mentioned in all four of the Gospels (*Dial.* c. 88).

But the most important fact mentioned in Justin's writings respecting these Memoirs, which he describes as "composed by Apostles of Christ and their companions," appears in his account of Christian worship, in the sixty-seventh chapter of his First Apology. "On the day called Sunday," he says, "all who live in cities or in the country gather together to one place, and the Memoirs by the Apostles or the writings of the Prophets are read, as long as time permits. When the reader has finished, the president admonishes and exhorts to the imitation of these good things." It appears, then, that, at the time when he wrote, these books, whatever they were, on which he relied for his knowledge of Christ's teaching and life, were held in at least as high reverence as the writings of the Prophets, were read in the churches just as our Gospels were in the last quarter of the second century, and formed the basis of the hortatory discourse that followed. The writings of the Prophets might alternate with them in this use; but Justin mentions the Memoirs first.

These "Memoirs," then, were well-known books, distin-

---

* I adopt with most scholars (*versus* Semisch and Grimm) the construction which refers the αὐτοῦ in this passage not to Christ, but to Peter, in accordance with the use of the genitive after ἀπομνημονεύματα everywhere else in Justin. (See a note on the question in the *Christian Examiner* for July, 1854, lvi. 128 f.) For the statement in the text, see Tertullian, *Adv. Marc.* iv. 5.: Licet et Marcus quod edidit [evangelium] Petri affirmetur, cujus interpres Marcus. Jerome, *De Vir. ill.* c. 1.: Sed et Evangelium juxta Marcum, qui auditor ejus [sc. Petri] et interpres fuit, hujus dicitur. Comp. *ibid.* c. 8, and *Ep.* 120 (al. 150) *ad Hedib.* c. 11. See also Papias, ap. Euseb. *Hist. Eccl.* iii. 39; Irenæus, *Hær.* iii. 1, § 1 (ap. Euseb. v. 8); 10, § 6; Clement of Alexandria ap. Euseb. ii. 15; vi. 14; Origen ap. Euseb. vi. 25; and the striking passage of Eusebius, *Dem. Evang.* iii. 3, pp. 120d–122a, quoted by Lardner, *Works* iv. 91 ff. (Lond. 1829).

guished from others as the authoritative source of instruction concerning the doctrine and life of Christ.

There is one other coincidence between the language which Justin uses in describing these books and that which we find in the generation following. The four Gospels as a collection might indifferently be called, and were indifferently cited as, "the Gospels" or "the Gospel." We find this use of the expression "the Gospel" in Theophilus of Antioch, Irenæus, Clement of Alexandria, Origen, Hippolytus, the Apostolical Constitutions, Tertullian, and later writers generally.* Now Justin represents Trypho as saying, "I know that your precepts in what is called the Gospel (ἐν τῷ λεγομένῳ εὐαγγελίῳ) are so wonderful and great as to cause a suspicion that no one may be able to observe them." (*Dial.* c. 10.) In another place, he quotes, apparently, Matt. xi. 27 (comp. Luke x. 22) as being "written in the Gospel."† No plausible explanation can be given of this language except that which recognizes in it the same usage that we constantly find in later Christian writers. The books which in one place Justin calls "Gospels," books composed by Apostles and their companions, were in reference to what gave them their distinctive value *one*. They were the record of the Gospel of Christ in different forms. No *one* of our present Gospels, if these were in circulation in the time of Justin, and certainly no *one* of that great number of Gospels which

---

* See Justin or Pseudo-Justin, *De Res.* c. 10.—Ignat. or Pseudo-Ignat. *Ad Philad.* cc. 5, 8; *Smyrn.* cc. 5(?), 7.—Pseudo-Clem. 2 *Ep. ad Cor.* c. 8.—Theophil. iii. 14.—Iren. *Hær.* i. 7. §4; 8. §4; 20. §2; 27. §2. ii. 22. §5; 26. §2. iii. 5. §1; 9. §2; 10. §§2, 6; 11. §§8 (τετράμορφον τὸ εὐαγγέλιον), 9; 16. §5. iv. 20. §§6, 9; 32. §1; 34. §1.—Clem. Al. *Pæd.* i. c. 5, pp. 104, 105, *bis* ed. Potter; c. 9, pp. 143, 145 *bis*, 148. ii. 1, p. 169; c. 10, p. 235; c. 12, p. 246. *Strom.* ii. 16, p. 467. iii. 6, p. 537; c. 11, p. 544. iv. 1, p. 564; c. 4, p. 570. v. 5, p. 664. vi. 6, p. 764; c. 11, p. 784 *bis*; c. 14, p. 797. vii. 3, p. 836. *Ecl. proph.* cc. 50, 57.—Origen, *Cont. Cels.* i. 51. ii. 13, 24, 27, 34, 36, 37, 61, 63 (Opp. I. 367, 398, 409, 411, 415, 416 *bis*, 433, 434 ed. Delarue). *In Joan.* tom. i. §§4, 5. v. §4. (Opp. IV. 4, 98.) Pseudo-Orig. *Dial. de recta in Deum fide*, sect. 1 (Opp. I. 807).—Hippol. *Noët.* c. 6.—Const. Ap. i. 1, 2 *bis*, 5, 6. ii. 1 *bis*, 5 *bis*, 6 *bis*, 8, 13, 16, 17, 35, 39. iii. 7. v. 14. vi. 23 *bis*, 28. vii. 24.—Tertull. *Cast.* c. 4. *Pudic.* c. 2. *Adv. Marc.* iv. 7. *Hermog.* c. 20. *Resurr.* c. 27. *Prax.* cc. 20, 21.—PLURAL, Muratorian Canon (also the sing.).—Theophilus, *Ad Autol.* iii. 12, τὰ τῶν προφητῶν καὶ τῶν εὐαγγελίων.—Clem. Al. Strom. iv. 6. p. 582. Hippol. *Ref. Hær.* vii. 38, p. 259, τῶν δὲ εὐαγγελίων ἢ τοῦ ἀποστόλου, and later writers everywhere.—*Plural* used where the passage quoted is found in only *one* of the Gospels, Basilides ap. Hippol. *Ref. Hær.* vii. 22, 27.—Const. Ap. ii. 53.—Cyril of Jerusalem, *Procat.* c. 3; *Cat.* ii. 4; x. 1; xvi. 16.—Theodoret, *Quæst. in Num.* c. xix. q. 35, Migne lxxx. 385; *In Ps.* xlv. 16, M. lxxx. 1197; *In 1 Thess.* v. 15, M. lxxxii. 649, and so often.

† On this important passage see Note A at the end of this essay.

the writer of *Supernatural Religion* imagines to have been current at that period, could have been so distinguished from the rest as to be called "*the* Gospel."

It has been maintained by the author of *Supernatural Religion* and others that Justin's description of the Gospels as "Memoirs composed by *the* Apostles and those who followed with them" (to render the Greek verbally) cannot apply to works composed by *two* Apostles and two companions of Apostles: "*the* Apostles" must mean *all* the Apostles, "the collective body of the Apostles." (*S. R.* i. 291.) Well, if it must, then the connected expression, "those that followed with them" (τῶν ἐκείνοις παρακολουθησάντων), where the definite article is used in just the same way in Greek, must mean "all those that followed with them." We have, then, a truly marvellous book, if we take the view of *Supernatural Religion* that the "Memoirs" of Justin was a single work; a Gospel, namely, composed by "the collective body of the Apostles" and the collective body of those who accompanied them. If the "Memoirs" consist of several different books *thus* composed, the marvel is not lessened. Now Justin is not responsible for this absurdity. The simple fact is that the definite article in Greek in this case distinguishes the two *classes* to which the writers of the Gospels belonged.*

To state in full detail and with precision all the features of the problem presented by Justin's quotations, and his references to facts in the life of Christ, is here, of course, impossible. But what is the obvious aspect of the case?

It will not be disputed that there is a very close correspondence between the history of Christ sketched by Justin, embracing numerous details, and that found in our Gospels: the few statements not authorized by them, such as that Christ was born in a cave, that the Magi came from Arabia, that Christ as a carpenter made ploughs and yokes,

* For illustrations of this use of the article, see Norton's *Evidences of the Genuineness of the Gospels*, 1st ed. (1837), vol. i. p. 190, note. Comp. 1 Thess. ii. 14 and Jude 17, where it would be idle to suppose that the writer means that *all* the Apostles had given the particular warning referred to. See also Origen, *Cont. Cels.* i. 51, p. 367, μετὰ τὴν ἀναγεγραμμένην ἐν τοῖς εὐαγγελίοις ὑπὸ τῶν Ἰησοῦ μαθητῶν ἱστορίαν; and ii. 13, παραπλήσια τοῖς ὑπὸ τῶν μαθητῶν τοῦ Ἰησοῦ γραφεῖσιν. Add *Cont. Cels.* ii. 16 init. See, further Note B at the end of this essay.

present little or no objection to the supposition that they were his main authority. These details may be easily explained as founded on oral tradition, or as examples of that substitution of *inferences* from facts for the facts themselves, which we find in so many ancient and modern writers, and observe in every-day life.* Again, there is a substantial correspondence between the teaching of Christ as reported by Justin and that found in the Gospels. Only one or two sayings are ascribed to Christ by Justin which are not contained in the Gospels, and these may naturally be referred, like others which we find in writers who received our four Gospels as alone authoritative, to oral tradition, or may have been taken from some writing or writings now lost which contained such traditions.† That Justin actually used all our present Gospels is admitted by Hilgenfeld and Keim. But that they were not his main authority is argued chiefly from the want of exact verbal correspondence between his citations of the words of Christ and the language of our Gospels, where the meaning is essentially the same. The untenableness of this argument has been demonstrated, I conceive, by Norton, Semisch, Westcott, and Sanday, *versus* Hilgenfeld and *Supernatural Religion*. Its weakness is illustrated in a Note at the end of this essay, and will be further illustrated presently by the full discussion of a passage of special interest and importance. Justin nowhere expressly

* Several of Justin's additions in the way of detail seem to have proceeded from his *assumption* of the fulfilment of Old Testament prophecies, or what he regarded as such. See Semisch, *Die apost. Denkwürdigkeiten des Märtyrers Justinus* (1848), p. 377 ff.; Volkmar, *Der Ursprung unserer Evangelien* (1866), p. 124 f.; Westcott, *Canon of the N. T.*, p. 162, 4th ed. (1875), and Dr. E. A. Abbott, art. *Gospels* in the ninth ed. of the Encyclopædia Britannica (p. 817), who remarks: "Justin never quotes any rival Gospel, nor alleges any words or facts which make it probable he used a rival Gospel; such non-canonical sayings and facts as he mentions are readily explicable as the results of lapse of memory, general looseness and inaccuracy, extending to the use of the Old as well as the New Testament, and the desire to adapt the facts of the New Scriptures to the prophecies of the Old." (p. 818).

† See Westcott, "On the Apocryphal Traditions of the Lord's Words and Works," appended to his *Introd. to the Study of the Gospels*, 5th ed. (1875), pp. 453-461, and the little volume of J. T. Dodd, *Sayings ascribed to our Lord by the Fathers*, etc., Oxford, 1874. Compare Norton, *Genuineness of the Gospels*, 2d ed., i. 220 ff. The stress which the author of *Supernatural Religion* lays on the word πάντα in the passage (*Apol.* i 33) where Justin speaks of "those who have written memoirs of *all things* concerning our Saviour Jesus Christ" shows an extraordinary disregard of the common use of such expressions. It is enough to compare, as Westcott does, Acts i. 1. For illustrations from Justin (*Apol.* ii. 6; i. 45; *Dial.* cc. 44, 121) see Semisch, *Die apost. Denkwürdigkeiten* u. s. w., p. 404 f.

quotes the "Memoirs" for anything which is not substantially found in our Gospels; and there is nothing in his deviations from exact correspondence with them, as regards matters of fact, or the report of the words of Christ, which may not be abundantly paralleled in the writings of the Christian Fathers who used our four Gospels as alone authoritative.

With this view of the state of the case, and of the character of the books used and described by Justin though without naming their authors, let us now consider the bearing of the indisputable fact (with which the author of *Supernatural Religion* thinks he has no concern) of the general reception of our four Gospels as genuine in the last quarter of the second century. As I cannot state the argument more clearly or more forcibly than it has been done by Mr. Norton, I borrow his language. Mr. Norton says:—

The manner in which Justin speaks of the character and authority of the books to which he appeals, of their reception among Christians, and of the use which was made of them, proves these books to have been the Gospels. They carried with them the authority of the Apostles. They were those writings from which he and other Christians derived their knowledge of the history and doctrines of Christ. They were relied upon by him as primary and decisive evidence in his explanations of the character of Christianity. They were regarded as sacred books. They were read in the assemblies of Christians on the Lord's day, in connection with the Prophets of the Old Testament. Let us now consider the manner in which the Gospels were regarded by the contemporaries of Justin. Irenæus was in the vigor of life before Justin's death; and the same was true of very many thousands of Christians living when Irenæus wrote. But he tells us that the four Gospels are the four pillars of the Church, the foundation of Christian faith, written by those who had first orally preached the Gospel, by two Apostles and two companions of Apostles. It is incredible that Irenæus and Justin should have spoken of different books. We cannot suppose that writings, such as the Memoirs of which Justin speaks, believed to be the works of Apostles and companions of Apostles, read in Christian Churches, and received as sacred books, of the highest authority, should, immediately after he wrote, have fallen into neglect and oblivion, and been superseded by another set of books. The strong sentiment of their value could not so silently, and so unaccountably, have changed into entire disregard, and have been transferred to other writings. The copies of them spread over the world could not so suddenly and mysteriously have disappeared, that no subsequent trace of their existence should be clearly discoverable. When, therefore, we find Irenæus, the contemporary of Justin, ascribing to the four Gospels the same character, the same authority, and the same authors, as are ascribed by Justin to the Memoirs quoted by him, which were called Gospels, there can be no reasonable doubt that the Memoirs of Justin were the Gospels of Irenæus.*

It may be objected to Mr. Norton's argument, that "many writings which have been excluded from the canon were publicly read in the churches, until very long after Justin's day." (*S.R.* i. 294.) The author of *Supernatural Religion* mentions particularly the Epistle of the Roman Clement to the Corinthians, the Epistle of Soter, the Bishop of Rome, to the Corinthians, the "Pastor" or "Shepherd" of Hermas, and the Apocalypse of Peter. To these may be added the Epistle ascribed to Barnabas.

To give the objection any force, the argument must run thus: The writings above named were at one time generally regarded by Christians as sacred books, of the highest authority and importance, and placed at least on a level with the writings of the prophets of the Old Testament. They were afterwards excluded from the canon: therefore a similar change might take place among Christians in their estimate of the writings which Justin has described under the name of "Memoirs by the Apostles." In the course of thirty years, a different set of books might silently supersede them in the whole Christian world.

The premises are false. There is no proof that any one of these writings was ever regarded as possessing the same authority and value as Justin's "Memoirs," or anything like it. From the very nature of the case, books received as authentic records of the life and teaching of CHRIST must have had an importance which could belong to no others. On the character of the teaching and the facts of the life of Christ as recorded in the "Memoirs," Justin's whole argument rests. Whether he regarded the Apostolic writings as "inspired" or not, he unquestionably regarded CHRIST as inspired, or rather as the divine, inspiring Logos (*Apol.* i.

* *Evidences of the Genuineness of the Gospels*, 2d ed., vol. i. pp. 237-239.

33, 36; ii. 10); and his teaching as "the new law," universal, everlasting, which superseded "the old covenant." (See *Dial.* cc. 11, 12, etc.) The books that contained this were to the Christians of Justin's time the very foundation of their faith.

As to the works mentioned by *Supernatural Religion*, not only is there no evidence that any one of them ever held a place in the Christian Church to be compared for a moment with that of the Gospels, but there is abundant evidence to the contrary. They were read in some churches for a time as edifying books,—the Epistle of Clement of Rome "in very many churches" according to Eusebius (*Hist. Eccl.* iii. 16),*—and a part of them were regarded by a few Christian writers as having apostolic or semi-apostolic authority, or as divinely inspired. One of the most definite statements about them is that of Dionysius of Corinth (*cir.* A.D. 175–180), who, in a letter to the church at Rome (Euseb. *Hist. Eccl.* iv. 23), tells us that the Epistle of Soter (d. 176?) to the Christians at Corinth was read in their church for edification or "admonition" (νουθετεῖσθαι is the word used) on a certain Sunday, and would continue to be so read from time to time, as the Epistle of Clement had been. This shows how far the occasional public reading of such a writing in the church was from implying its canonical authority.—Clement of Alexandria repeatedly quotes the Epistle ascribed to Barnabas as the work of "Barnabas the Apostle," but criticises and condemns one of his interpretations (*Strom.* ii. 15, p. 464), and in another place, as Mr. Norton remarks, rejects a fiction found in the work (*Pæd.* ii. 10, p. 220, ff.).—"The Shepherd" of Hermas in its *form* claims to be a divine vision; its allegorical character suited the taste of many; and the Muratorian Canon (*cir.* A.D. 170) says that it ought to be read in the churches, but not as belonging to the writings of the prophets or apostles. (See Credner, *Gesch. d. neutest. Kanon*, p. 165.) This was the general view of those who did not reject it as altogether apocryphal. It appears in the Sinaitic MS. as an appendix to the New Testament.—The Apocalypse of Peter appears to have imposed upon some

* Comp. esp. Lightfoot, *Clement of Rome*, p. 272 ff.

as the work of the Apostle. The Muratorian Canon says, "Some among us are unwilling that it should be read in the church." It seems to have been received as genuine by Clement of Alexandria (*Ecl. proph.* cc. 41, 48, 49) and Methodius (*Conv.* ii. 6). Besides these, the principal writers who speak of it are Eusebius (*Hist. Eccl.* iii. 3. § 2; 25. § 4; vi. 14. § 1), who rejects it as uncanonical or spurious, Jerome (*De Vir. ill.* c. 1), who puts it among apocryphal writings, and Sozomen (*Hist. Eccl.* vii. 19), who mentions that, though rejected by the ancients as spurious, it was read once a year in some churches of Palestine.*

It appears sufficiently from what has been said that there is nothing in the limited ecclesiastical use of these books, or in the over-estimate of their authority and value by some individuals, to detract from the force of Mr. Norton's argument. *Supernatural Religion* here confounds things that differ very widely.†

At this stage of the argument, we are entitled, I think, to come to the examination of the apparent use of the Gospel of John by Justin Martyr with a strong presumption in favor of the view that this apparent use is real. In other words, there is a very strong presumption that the "Memoirs" used by Justin and called by him "Gospels" and collectively "the Gospel," and described as "composed by Apostles of Christ and their companions," were actually our present Gospels, composed by two Apostles and two companions of Apostles. This presumption is, I believe, greatly strengthened by the evidence of the use of the Fourth Gospel by writers between the time of Justin Martyr and Irenæus, and also by the evidences of its use before the time of Justin by the Gnostic sects. But, leaving those topics for the present, we will consider the direct evidence of its use by Justin.

The first passage noticed will be examined pretty thoroughly: both because the discussion of it will serve to illustrate the false reasoning of the author of *Supernatural Relig-*

---

* See, on this book, Hilgenfeld, *Nov. Test. extra canonem receptum* (1866), iv. 74, ff.

† On this whole subject, see Semisch, *Die apostol. Denkwürdigkeiten des Märt. Justinus*, p. 61, ff.

ion and other writers respecting the quotations of Justin Martyr which agree in substance with passages in our Gospels while differing in the form of expression; and because it is of special importance in its bearing on the question whether Justin made use of the Fourth Gospel, and seems to me, when carefully examined, to be in itself almost decisive.

The passage is that in which Justin gives an account of Christian baptism, in the sixty-first chapter of his First Apology. Those who are ready to make a Christian profession, he says, "are brought by us to a place where there is water, and in the manner of being born again [*or* regenerated] in which we ourselves also were born again, they are born again; for in the name of the Father of the universe and sovereign God, and of our Saviour Jesus Christ, and of the Holy Spirit, they then receive the bath in the water. For Christ also said, Except ye be born again, ye shall in no wise enter into the kingdom of heaven (Ἂν μὴ ἀναγεννηθῆτε, οὐ μὴ εἰσέλθητε εἰς τὴν βασιλείαν τῶν οὐρανῶν). But that it is impossible for those who have once been born to enter into the wombs of those who brought them forth is manifest to all."

The passage in the Gospel of John of which this reminds us is found in chap. iii. 3–5: "Jesus answered and said to him [Nicodemus], Verily, verily I say unto thee, Except a man be born anew, he cannot see the kingdom of God (Ἐὰν μή τις γεννηθῇ ἄνωθεν, οὐ δύναται ἰδεῖν τὴν βασιλείαν τοῦ Θεοῦ). Nicodemus saith to him, How can a man be born when he is old? Can he enter a second time into his mother's womb and be born? Jesus answered, Verily, verily I say unto thee, Except a man be born of water and the Spirit, he cannot enter into the kingdom of God" (Ἐὰν μή τις γεννηθῇ ἐξ ὕδατος καὶ πνεύματος, οὐ δύναται εἰσελθεῖν εἰς τὴν βασιλείαν τοῦ Θεοῦ). Compare verse 7, "Marvel not that I said unto thee, Ye must be born anew" (δεῖ ὑμᾶς γεννηθῆναι ἄνωθεν); and Matt. xviii. 3, "Verily I say unto you, Except ye be changed, and become as little children, ye shall in no wise enter into the kingdom of heaven" (οὐ μὴ εἰσέλθητε εἰς τὴν βασιλείαν τῶν οὐρανῶν).

I have rendered the Greek as literally as possible; but it

should be observed that the word translated "anew," ἄνωθεν, might also be rendered "from above." This point will be considered hereafter.

Notwithstanding the want of verbal correspondence, I believe that we have here in Justin a free quotation from the Gospel of John, modified a little by a reminiscence of Matt. xviii. 3.

The first thing that strikes us in Justin's quotation is the fact that the remark with which it concludes, introduced by Justin as if it were a grave observation of his own, is simply silly in the connection in which it stands. In John, on the other hand, where it is not to be understood as a serious question, it admits, as we shall see, of a natural explanation as the language of Nicodemus. This shows, as everything else shows, the weakness (to use no stronger term) of Volkmar's hypothesis, that John has here borrowed from Justin, not Justin from John. The observation affords also, by its very remarkable peculiarity, strong evidence that Justin derived it, together with the declaration which accompanies it, from the Fourth Gospel.

It will be well, before proceeding to our immediate task, to consider the meaning of the passage in John, and what the real difficulty of Nicodemus was. He could not have been perplexed by the figurative use of the expression "to be born anew": that phraseology was familiar to the Jews to denote the change which took place in a Gentile when he became a proselyte to Judaism.* But the unqualified language of our Saviour, expressing a universal necessity, implied that even the Jewish Pharisee, with all his pride of sanctity and superior knowledge, must experience a radical change, like that which a Gentile proselyte to Judaism underwent, before he could enjoy the blessings of the Messiah's kingdom. This was what amazed Nicodemus. Pretending therefore to take the words in their literal meaning, he asks, "How can a man be born when he is old? Can he enter," etc. He imposes an absurd and ridiculous sense on the

* See Lightfoot and Wetstein, or T. Robinson or Wünsche, on John iii. 3 or 5.

words, to lead Jesus to explain himself further.* Thus viewed, the question is to some purpose in John; while the language in Justin, as a serious proposition, is idle, and betrays its non-originality.

The great difference in the form of expression between Justin's citation and the Gospel of John is urged as decisive against the supposition that he has here used this Gospel. It is observed further that all the deviations of Justin from the language of the Fourth Gospel are also found in a quotation of the words of Christ in the Clementine Homilies; and hence it has been argued that Justin and the writer of the Clementines quoted from the same apocryphal Gospel, perhaps the Gospel according to the Hebrews or the Gospel according to Peter. In the Clementine Homilies (xi. 26), the quotation runs as follows: "For thus the prophet swore unto us, saying, Verily I say unto you, except ye be born again by living water into the name of Father, Son, Holy Spirit, ye shall in no wise enter into the kingdom of heaven." But it will be seen at once that the author of the Clementines differs as widely from Justin as Justin from the Fourth Gospel, and that there is no plausibility in the supposition that he and Justin quoted from the same apocryphal book. The quotation in the Clementines is probably only a free combination of the language in John iii. 3–5 with Matt. xxviii. 19, modified somewhat in form by the influence of Matt. xviii. 3.† Such combinations of different passages, and such quotations of the words of Christ according to the sense rather than the letter, are not uncommon in the Fathers. Or, the Clementines may have used Justin.‡

I now propose to show in detail that the differences in form between Justin's quotation and the phraseology of the Fourth Gospel, marked as they are, all admit of an easy and natural explanation on the supposition that he really borrowed from it, and that they are paralleled by similar variations in the

---

* See Norton, *A New Trans. of the Gospels, with Notes*, vol. ii. p. 507.

† On the quotations from the Gospel of John as well as from the other Gospels in the Clementine Homilies, see Sanday, *The Gospels in the Second Century*, pp. 288–295; comp. pp. 161–187. See also Westcott, *Canon of the N. T.*, pp. 282–288; and comp. pp. 150–156.

‡ So Bleek, *Beiträge*, p. 221; Anger, *Synopsis*, p. 273; De Wette, *Einl.* § 67*e*, note *g*. Comp. Keim, *Urchrist.*, p. 225, note, who asserts, in general, that Justin Martyr is "besonders benutzt" by the author of the Clementine Homilies.

quotations of the same passage by Christian writers who used our four Gospels as their exclusive authority. If this is made clear, the fallacy of the assumption on which the author of *Supernatural Religion* reasons in his remarks on this passage, and throughout his discussion of Justin's quotations, will be apparent. He has argued on an assumption of verbal accuracy in the quotations of the Christian Fathers which is baseless, and which there were peculiar reasons for not expecting from Justin in such works as his Apologies.*

Let us take up the differences point by point:—

1. The solemn introduction, "Verily, verily I say unto thee," is omitted. But this would be very naturally omitted: (1) because it is of no importance for the sense; and (2) because the Hebrew words used, Ἀμὴν ἀμήν, would be unintelligible to the Roman Emperor, without a particular explanation (compare *Apol.* i. 65). (3) It is usually omitted by Christian writers in quoting the passage: so, for example, by the DOCETIST in HIPPOLYTUS (*Ref. Hær.* viii. 10, p. 267), IRENÆUS (Frag. 35, ed. Stieren, 33 Harvey), ORIGEN, in a Latin version (*In Ex. Hom.* v. 1, Opp. ii. 144, ed. Delarue; *In Ep. ad Rom.* lib. v. c. 8, Opp. iv. 560), the APOSTOLICAL CONSTITUTIONS (vi. 15), EUSEBIUS twice (*In Isa.* i. 16, 17, and iii. 1, 2; Migne xxiv. 96, 109), ATHANASIUS (*De Incarn.* c. 14, Opp. i. 59, ed. Montf.), CYRIL OF JERUSALEM twice (*Cat.* iii. 4; xvii. 11), BASIL THE GREAT (*Adv. Eunom.* lib. v. Opp. i. 308 (437), ed. Benedict.), PSEUDO-BASIL three times (*De Bapt.* i. 2. §§ 2, 6; ii. 1. § 1; Opp. ii. 630 (896), 633 (899), 653 (925)), GREGORY NYSSEN (*De Christi Bapt.* Opp. iii. 369), EPHRAEM SYRUS (*De Pœnit.* Opp. iii. 183), MACARIUS ÆGYP-

* On the whole subject of Justin Martyr's quotations, I would refer to the admirably clear, forcible, and accurate statement of the case in Norton's *Evidences of the Genuineness of the Gospels*, 2d ed., vol. i. pp. 200–239, and Addit. Note E, pp. ccxiv.–ccxxxviii. His account is less detailed than that of Semisch, Hilgenfeld, and *Supernatural Religion*, but is thoroughly trustworthy. On one point there may be a doubt: Mr. Norton says that "Justin twice gives the words, *Thou art my son; this day have I begotten thee*, as those uttered at our Saviour's baptism; and in one place says expressly that the words were found in the Memoirs by the Apostles." This last statement seems to me incorrect. The quotations referred to will be found in *Dial. c. Tryph.* cc. 88, 103; but in neither case does Justin *say*, according to the grammatical construction of his language, that the words in question were found in the Memoirs, though it is probable that they were. (See below, p. 101 f.) The discussion of Justin's quotations by Prof. Westcott and Dr. Sanday in the works referred to in note † on the preceding page is also valuable, especially in reference to the early variations in the text of the Gospels.

TIUS (*Hom.* xxx. 3), CHRYSOSTOM (*De consubst.* vii. 3, Opp. i. 505 (618), ed. Montf.; *In Gen. Serm.* vii. 5, Opp. iv. 681 (789), and elsewhere repeatedly), THEODORET (*Quæst. in Num.* 35, Migne lxxx. 385), BASIL OF SELEUCIA (*Orat.* xxviii. 3, Migne lxxxv. 321), and a host of other writers, both Greek and Latin,—I could name *forty*, if necessary.

2. The change of the indefinite τις, in the singular, to the second person plural: "Except *a man* be born anew" to "Except *ye* be born anew." This also is unimportant. This is shown, and the origin of the change is partially explained (1) by the fact, not usually noticed, that it is made *by the speaker himself in the Gospel*, in professedly repeating in the seventh verse the words used in the third; the indefinite singular involving, and being equivalent to, the plural. Verse 7 reads: "Marvel not that I *said* unto thee, *Ye* must be born anew." (2) The second person plural would also be suggested by the similar passage in Matt. xviii. 3, "Except *ye* be changed and become as little children, *ye* shall in no wise enter into the kingdom of heaven." Nothing was more natural than that in a quotation from memory the language of these two kindred passages should be somewhat mixed; and such a confusion of similar passages is frequent in the writings of the Fathers. This affords an easy explanation also of Justin's substituting, in agreement with Matthew, "shall in no wise enter" for "cannot enter," and "kingdom of heaven" for "kingdom of God." The two passages of John and Matthew are actually mixed together in a somewhat similar way in a free quotation by CLEMENT OF ALEXANDRIA, a writer who unquestionably used our Gospels alone as authoritative,—"the four Gospels, which," as he says, "*have been handed down* to us" (*Strom.* iii. 13, p. 553).* (3) This declaration of Christ would often be quoted in the early Christian preaching, in reference to the importance of baptism; and the second person plural would thus be natu-

---

* Clement (*Cohort. ad Gentes*, c. 9, p. 69) blends Matt. xviii. 3 and John iii. 3 as follows: "Except ye again become as little children, and *be born again* (ἀναγεννηθῆτε), as the Scripture saith, ye will in no wise receive him who is truly your Father, and will in no wise ever enter into the kingdom of heaven."

rally substituted for the indefinite singular, to give greater directness to the exhortation. So in the CLEMENTINE HOMILIES (xi. 26), and in both forms of the CLEMENTINE EPITOME (c. 18, pp. 16, 134, ed. Dressel, Lips. 1859). (4) That this change of number and person does not imply the use of an apocryphal Gospel is further shown by the fact that it is made twice in quoting the passage by Jeremy Taylor, who in a third quotation also substitutes the plural for the singular in a somewhat different way.* (See below, p. 42.)

3. The change of ἐὰν μή τις γεννηθῇ ἄνωθεν, verse 3 (or γεννηθῇ merely, verse 5), "Except a man be born anew," or "over again," into ἂν μὴ ἀναγεννηθῆτε, "Except ye be born again," or "regenerated"; in other words, the substitution of ἀναγεννᾶσθαι for γεννᾶσθαι ἄνωθεν, or for the simple verb in verse 5, presents no real difficulty, though much has been made of it. (1) It is said that γεννᾶσθαι ἄνωθεν cannot mean "to be born *anew*," but must mean "to be born *from above*." But we have the clearest philological evidence that ἄνωθεν has the meaning of "anew," "over again," as well as "from above." In the only passage in a classical author where the precise phrase, γεννᾶσθαι ἄνωθεν, has been pointed out, namely, Artemidorus on Dreams, i. 13, ed. Reiff (al. 14), it cannot possibly have any other meaning. Meyer, who rejects this sense, has fallen into a strange mistake about the passage in Artemidorus, showing that he cannot have looked at it. Meaning "from above" or "from the top" (Matt. xxvii. 51), then "from the beginning" (Luke i. 3), ἄνωθεν is used, with πάλιν to strengthen

* Professor James Drummond well remarks: "How easily such a change might be made, when verbal accuracy was not studied, is instructively shewn in Theophylact's paraphrase [I translate the Greek]: 'But I say unto thee, that both thou and every other man whatsoever, unless having been born from above [*or* anew] and of God, *ye* receive the true faith [*lit.* the worthy opinion] concerning me, are outside of the kingdom.'" Chrysostom (also cited by Prof. Drummond) observes that Christ's words are equivalent to ἐὰν σὺ μὴ γεννηθῇ κ.τ.λ., "Except *thou* be born," etc., but are put in the indefinite form in order to make the discourse less offensive. Photius, in quoting John iii. 5, substitutes ὑμῖν for σοί. (See below, p. 36.) I gladly take this opportunity to call attention to the valuable article by Prof. Drummond in the *Theological Review* for October, 1875, vol. vii. pp. 471–488, "On the alleged Quotation from the Fourth Gospel relating to the New Birth, in Justin Martyr, *Apol.* i. c. 61." He has treated the question with the ability, candor, and cautious accuracy of statement which distinguish his writings generally. For the quotation given above, see p. 476 of the *Review*. I am indebted to him for several valuable suggestions; but, to prevent misapprehension as to the extent of this indebtedness, I may be permitted to refer to my note on the subject in the American edition of Smith's *Dictionary of the Bible*, vol. ii. p. 1433, published in 1869, six years before the appearance of Prof. Drummond's article.

it, to signify "again from the beginning," "all over again" (Gal. iv. 9, where see the passages from Galen and Hippocrates cited by Wetstein, and Wisd. of Sol. xix. 6, where see Grimm's note), like πάλιν ἐκ δευτέρου or δεύτερον (Matt. xxvi. 42, John xxi. 16), and in the classics πάλιν αὖ, πάλιν αὖθις, πάλιν ἐξ ἀρχῆς. Thus it gets the meaning "anew," "over again"; see the passages cited by McClellan in his note on John iii. 3.* (2) Ἄνωθεν was here understood as meaning "again" by the translators of many of the ancient versions; namely, the Old Latin, "denuo," the Vulgate, Coptic, Peshito Syriac (*Sup. Rel.*, 6th edit., is mistaken about this), Æthiopic, Georgian (see Malan's *The Gospel according to St. John*, etc.). (3) The Christian Fathers who prefer the other interpretation, as Origen, Cyril of Alexandria, and Theophylact, recognize the fact that the word may have either meaning. The ambiguity is also noticed by Chrysostom. (4) Ἀναγεννᾶσθαι was the common word in Christian literature to describe the change referred to. So already in 1 Pet. i. 3, 23; comp. 1 Pet. ii. 2; and see the context in Justin. (5) This meaning best suits the connection. Verse 4 represents it as so understood by Nicodemus: "Can he enter *a second time*," etc. The fact that John has used the word ἄνωθεν in two other passages in a totally different connection (viz. iii. 31, xix. 11) in the sense of "from above" is of little weight. He has nowhere else used it in reference to the new birth to denote that it is a birth from above: to express that idea, he has used a differ-

*The passages are: Joseph. *Ant.* i. 18, § 3; Socrates in Stobæus, *Flor.* cxxiv. 41, iv. 135 Meineke; Harpocration, *Lex.* s. v. ἀναδικάσασθαι; Pseudo-Basil, *De Bapt.* i. 2. § 7; Can. Apost. 46, al. 47, al. 39; to which add Origen, *In Joan.* tom. xx. c. 12, Opp. iv. 322, who gives the words of Christ to Peter in the legend found in the Acts of Paul: ἄνωθεν μέλλω σταυρωθῆναι = "*iterum* crucifigi." I have verified McClellan's references (*The N.T.* etc. vol. 1. p. 284, Lond. 1875), and given them in a form in which they may be more easily found.

Though many of the best commentators take ἄνωθεν here in the sense of "from above," as Bengel, Lücke, De Wette, Meyer, Clausen, and so the lexicographers Wahl, Bretschneider, Robinson, the rendering "anew" is supported by Chrysostom, Nonnus, Euthymius, Budæus, Henry Stephen (*Thes.* s. v.), Luther, Calvin, Beza, Grotius, Wetstein, Kypke, Krebs, Knapp (*Scripta var. Arg.* i. 188, ed. 2da), Kuinoel, Credner (*Beiträge*, i. 253), Olshausen, Tholuck, Neander, Norton, Noyes, Alford, Ewald, Hofmann, Hengstenberg, Luthardt, Weiss, Godet, Farrar, Watkins, Westcott, and the recent lexicographers, Grimm and Cremer. The word is not to be understood as merely equivalent to "again," "a second time," but implies an entire change. Compare the use of εἰς τέλος in the sense of "completely," and the Ep. of Barnabas, c. 16, § 8 (cited by Bretschneider): "Having received the forgiveness of our sins, and having placed our hope in the Name, we became new men, created again from the beginning" (πάλιν ἐξ ἀρχῆς).

ent expression, γεννηθῆναι ἐκ θεοῦ or ἐκ τοῦ θεοῦ, "to be born [*or* begotten] of God," which occurs once in the Gospel (i. 13) and nine times in the First Epistle, so that the presumption is that, if he had wished to convey that meaning here, he would have used here also that unambiguous expression.

But what is decisive as to the main point is the fact that Justin's word ἀναγεννηθῇ is actually substituted for γεννηθῇ ἄνωθεν in verse 3, or for the simple γεννηθῇ in verse 5, by a large number of Christian writers who unquestionably quote from John; so, besides the CLEMENTINE HOMILIES (xi. 26) and the CLEMENTINE EPITOME in both forms (c. 18), to which exception has been taken with no sufficient reason, IRENÆUS (Frag. 35, ed. Stieren, i. 846), EUSEBIUS (*In Isa.* i. 16, 17; Migne xxiv. 96), ATHANASIUS (*De Incarn.* c. 14), BASIL (*Adv. Eunom.* lib. v. Opp. i. 308 (437)), EPHRAEM SYRUS (*De Pœnit.* Opp. iii. 183 (ἀναγεννηθῇ ἄνωθεν)), CHRYSOSTOM (*In* 1 *Ep. ad Cor.* xv. 29, Opp. x. 378 (440)),* CYRIL OF ALEXANDRIA (*In Joan.* iii. 5. ἐξαναγεννηθῇ δι' ὕδατος κ.τ.λ., so Pusey's critical ed., vol. i. p. 219; Aubert has γεννηθῇ ἐξ ὕδ.); PROCOPIUS GAZÆUS, *Comm. in Is.* i. 20 (Migne lxxxvii. 1849[a b]): ἐὰν μή τις ἀναγεννηθῇ ἐξ ὕδατος καὶ πνεύματος οὐ μὴ εἰσέλθῃ εἰς τὴν βασιλείαν τῶν οὐρανῶν; PHOTIUS, *Ad Amphiloch.* Q. 49 (al. 48) (Migne ci. 369[c]): ὁ σωτὴρ . . . ἔλεγεν· 'Αμήν, ἀμὴν λέγω ὑμῖν· ἐὰν μή τις ἀναγεννηθῇ δι' ὕδατος καὶ πνεύματος, οὐκ εἰσελεύσεται εἰς τὴν βασιλείαν τῶν οὐρανῶν; and so, probably, ANASTASIUS SINAITA preserved in a Latin version (*Anagog. Contemp. in Hexaëm.* lib. iv., Migne lxxxix. 906, *regeneratus*; contra, col. 870, *genitus*, 916, *generatus*), and HESYCHIUS OF JERUSALEM in a Latin version (*In Levit.* xx. 9, Migne xciii. 1044, *regeneratus*; but col. 974, *renatus*). In the Old Latin version or versions and the Vulgate, the MSS. are divided in John iii. 3 between *natus* and *renatus*, and so in verse 4, 2d clause, between *nasci* and *renasci*; but in verse 5 *renatus fuerit* is the unquestionable reading of the Latin versions, presupposing, apparently, ἀναγεννηθῇ in the Greek. (See Tischendorf's 8th critical edition of the Greek Test. *in loc.*) The Latin Fathers, with the exception of Tertullian and Cyprian, who have both readings, and of the author *De Rebaptismate* (c. 3), in quoting the passage, almost invariably have *renatus*.

---

* Comp. CHRYSOSTOM, *De Sacerdot.* iii. 5, Opp. i. 383[c] (469), cited by Westcott, *Canon of the N. T.*, 5th ed., 1881, p. xxx., note 1, § 3.

We occasionally find ἀναγεννηθῆναι, "to be born again," for γεννηθῆναι, "to be born," in the first clause of verse 4; so EPHRAEM SYRUS (*De Pœnit.* Opp. iii. 183), and CYRIL OF ALEXANDRIA (*Glaph. in Exod.* lib. iii., Opp. i. a. 341).

From all that has been said, it will be seen that the use of ἀναγεννηθῆτε here by Justin is easily explained. Whether ἄνωθεν in John really means "from above" or "anew" is of little importance in its bearing on our question: there can be no doubt that Justin *may* have understood it in the latter sense; and, even if he did not, the use of the term ἀναγεννᾶσθαι here was very natural, as is shown by the way in which the passage is quoted by Irenæus, Eusebius, and many other writers.

4. The next variation, the change of "*cannot* see" or "enter into" (οὐ δύναται ἰδεῖν or εἰσελθεῖν εἰς, *Lat.* non potest videre, *or* intrare *or* introire in) into "*shall* not" or "*shall in no wise* see" or "enter into" (οὐ μὴ ἴδῃ, once ἴδοι, or οὐ μὴ εἰσέλθῃ or εἰσέλθητε εἰς, twice οὐκ εἰσελεύσεται εἰς, *Lat.* non videbit, *or* intrabit *or* introibit in), is both so natural (comp. Matt. xviii. 3) and so trivial as hardly to deserve mention. It is perhaps enough to say that I have noted *seventy-one* examples of it in the quotations of this passage by *forty-four* different writers among the Greek and Latin Fathers. It is to be observed that in most of the quotations of the passage by the Fathers, verses 3 and 5 are mixed in different ways, as might be expected.

5. The change of "kingdom of *God*" into "kingdom of *heaven*" is perfectly natural, as they are synonymous expressions, and as the phrase "kingdom of heaven" is used in the passage of Matthew already referred to, the language of which was likely to be more or less confounded in recollection with that of this passage in John. The change is actually made in several Greek MSS. in the 5th verse of John, including the Sinaitic, and is even received by Tischendorf into the text, though, I believe, on insufficient grounds. But a great number of Christian writers in quoting from John make just the same change; so the DOCETIST in HIPPOLYTUS (*Ref. Hær.* viii. 10, p. 267), the CLEMENTINE HOMILIES (xi. 26), the RECOGNITIONS (i. 69; vi. 9), the CLEMENTINE EPITOME (c. 18) in both forms, IRENÆUS (Frag. 35, ed. Stieren), ORIGEN in a Latin version twice (*Opp.* iii. 948; iv. 483), the APOSTOLICAL CONSTITUTIONS (vi. 15), EUSEBIUS

twice (*In Isa.* i. 16, 17; iii. 1, 2; Migne xxiv. 96, 109), PSEUD-ATHANASIUS (*Quæst. ad Antioch.* 101, Opp. ii. 291), EPHRAEM SYRUS (*De Pœnit.* Opp. iii. 183), CHRYSOSTOM five or six times (*Opp.* iv. 681 (789); viii. 143de (165), 144[d] (165), 144[b] (166)), THEODORET (*Quæst. in Num.* 35, Migne lxxx. 385), BASIL OF SELEUCIA (*Orat.* xxviii. 3), PROCOPIUS, PHOTIUS, ANASTASIUS SINAITA in a Latin version three times (Migne lxxxix. 870, 906, 916), HESYCHIUS OF JERUSALEM in a Latin version twice (Migne xciii. 974, 1044), THEODORUS ABUCARA (*Opuscc.* c. 17, Migne xcvii. 1541), TERTULLIAN (*De Bapt.* c. 13), ANON. *De Rebaptismate* (c. 3), PHILASTRIUS (*Hær.* 120 and 148, ed. Oehler), CHROMATIUS (*In Matt.* iii. 14, Migne xx. 329), JEROME twice (*Ep.* 69, al. 83, and *In Isa.* i. 16; Migne xxii. 660, xxv. 35), AUGUSTINE seven times (*Opp.* ii. 1360, 1361; v. 1745; vi. 327; vii. 528; ix. 630; x. 207, ed. Bened. 2da), and a host of other Latin Fathers.

It should be observed that many of the writers whom I have cited *combine* three or four of these variations from John. It may be well to give, further, some additional illustrations of the freedom with which this passage is sometimes quoted and combined with others. One example has already been given from Clement of Alexandria. (See No. 2.) TERTULLIAN (*De Bapt.* 12) quotes it thus: "The Lord says, Except a man shall be born of water, he *hath not life*,"—Nisi natus ex aqua quis erit, non *habet vitam.* Similarly ODO CLUNIACENSIS (*Mor. in Job.* iii. 4, Migne cxxxiii. 135): "Veritas autem dicit, Nisi quis *renatus* fuerit ex aqua et Spiritu *sancto*, non *habet vitam æternam.*" ANASTASIUS SINAITA, as preserved in a Latin version (*Anagog. Contempl. in Hexaëm.* lib. v., Migne lxxxix. 916), quotes the passage as follows: "dicens, Nisi quis fuerit generatus ex aqua et Spiritu *qui fertur super aquam*, non *intrabit in* regnum *cælorum.*" The APOSTOLICAL CONSTITUTIONS (vi. 15) as edited by Cotelier and Ueltzen read: "For the Lord saith, Except a man be *baptized* with (βαπτισθῇ ἐξ) water and the Spirit, he *shall in no wise* enter into the kingdom of *heaven.*" Here, indeed, Lagarde, with two MSS., edits γεννηθῇ for βαπτισθῇ, but the more difficult reading may well be genuine. Compare EUTHYMIUS ZIGABENUS (*Panopl.* pars ii. tit. 23, Adv. Bogomilos, c 16, in the Latin version in Max. Bibl. Patrum, xix.

224), "Nisi quis *baptizatus* fuerit ex aqua et Spiritu *sancto*, non *intrabit in* regnum Dei," and see Jeremy Taylor, as quoted below. DIDYMUS OF ALEXANDRIA gives as the words of Christ (εἶπεν δέ), "Ye must be born *of water*" (*De Trin.* ii. 12, p. 250, Migne xxxix. 672). It will be seen that all these examples purport to be express quotations.

My principal object in this long discussion has been to show how false is the assumption on which the author of *Supernatural Religion* proceeds in his treatment of Justin's quotations, and those of other early Christian writers. But the fallacy of his procedure may, perhaps, be made more striking by some illustrations of the way in which the very passage of John which we have been considering is quoted by a modern English writer. I have noted nine quotations of the passage by Jeremy Taylor, who is not generally supposed to have used many apocryphal Gospels. All of these differ from the common English version, and only two of them are alike. They exemplify *all* the peculiarities of variation from the common text upon which the writers of the Tübingen school and others have laid such stress as proving that Justin cannot have here quoted John. I will number these quotations, with a reference to the volume and page in which they occur in Heber's edition of Jeremy Taylor's Works, London, 1828, 15 vols. 8vo, giving also such specifications as may enable one to find the passages in any other edition of his complete Works; and, without copying them all in full, will state their peculiarities. No. 1. Life of Christ, Part I. Sect. IX. Disc. VI. Of Baptism, part i. § 12. Heber, vol. ii. p. 240.— No. 2. *Ibid.* Disc. VI. Of baptizing Infants, part ii. § 26. Heber, ii. 288.— No. 3. *Ibid.* § 32. Heber, ii. 292.— No. 4. Liberty of Prophesying, Sect. XVIII. § 7. Heber, viii. 153.— No. 5. *Ibid.* Ad 7. Heber, viii. 190.— No. 6. *Ibid.* Ad 18. Heber, viii. 191.— No. 7. *Ibid.* Ad 18. Heber, viii. 193.— No. 8. Disc. of Confirm. Sect. I. Heber, xi. 238.— No. 9. *Ibid.* Heber, xi. 244.

We may notice the following points:—

1. He has "unless" for "except," uniformly. This is a trifling variation; but, reasoning after the fashion of *Super-*

natural Religion, we should say that this uniformity of variation could not be referred to accident, but proved that he quoted from a different text from that of the authorized version.

2. He has "kingdom of *heaven*" for "kingdom of *God*" six times; viz., Nos. 1, 2, 3, 4, 5, 7.

3. "*Heaven*" simply for "kingdom of God" once; No. 6.

4. "*Shall not* enter" for "*cannot* enter" four times; Nos. 4, 5, 7, 8; comp. also No. 6.

5. The second person plural, *ye*, for the third person singular, twice; Nos. 3, 7.

6. "*Baptized with* water" for "*born of* water" once; No. 7.

7. "Born *again by* water" for "born *of* water" once; No. 6.

8. "*Both of* water and the Spirit" for "*of* water and *of* the Spirit" once; No. 9.

9. "Of" is *omitted* before "the Spirit" six times; Nos. 1, 2, 3, 6, 7, 8.

10. "Holy" is *inserted* before "Spirit" twice; Nos. 1, 8.

No. 1 reads, for example, "*Unless* a man be born of water and the *Holy* Spirit, he cannot enter into the kingdom of *heaven*."

Supernatural Religion insists that, when Justin uses such an expression as "Christ said," we may expect a verbally accurate quotation.* Now nothing is more certain than that the Christian Fathers frequently use such a formula when they mean to give merely the substance of what Christ said, and not the exact words; but let us apply our author's principle to Jeremy Taylor. No. 3 of his quotations reads thus:

"Therefore our Lord hath defined it, *Unless ye* be born of water and the Spirit, *ye* cannot enter into the kingdom of *heaven*."

No. 6 reads, "Though Christ said, *None but those that are born again by* water and the Spirit *shall* enter into *heaven*."

No. 7 reads, "For Christ never said, *Unless ye be baptized*

---

* "Justin, in giving the words of Jesus, clearly professed to make an exact quotation."—*Supernatural Religion*, ii. 309, 7th ed.

with fire and the Spirit, *ye shall not* enter into the kingdom of *heaven*, but of water and the Spirit he *did say it*."

I will add one quotation from the Book of Common Prayer, which certainly must be quoting from another apocryphal Gospel, different from those used by Jeremy Taylor (he evidently had several), inasmuch as it professes to give the very words of Christ, and gives them *twice* in precisely the same form:—

"Our Saviour Christ saith, *None can* enter into the kingdom of God except he be *regenerate and* born *anew* of water and of the *Holy Ghost*." (*Public Baptism of Infants*, and *Baptism of those of Riper Years*.)

It has been shown, I trust, that in this quotation of the language of Christ respecting regeneration the verbal differences between Justin and John are not such as to render it improbable that the former borrowed from the latter. The variations of phraseology are easily accounted for, and are matched by similar variations in writers who unquestionably used the Gospel of John.

The positive reasons for believing that Justin derived his quotation from this source are, (1) the fact that in no other report of the teaching of Christ except that of John do we find this figure of the new birth; (2) the insistence in both Justin and John on the necessity of the new birth to an entrance into the kingdom of heaven; (3) its mention in both in connection with baptism; (4) and last and most important of all, the fact that Justin's remark on the impossibility of a second natural birth is such a platitude in the form in which he presents it, that we cannot regard it as original. We can only explain its introduction by supposing that the language of Christ which he quotes was strongly associated in his memory with the question of Nicodemus as recorded by John.* Other evidences of the use of the Fourth Gospel by Justin are the following:—

(*a*) While Justin's conceptions in regard to the Logos were undoubtedly greatly affected by Philo and the Alexandrian

* Engelhardt in his recent work on Justin observes: "This remark sets aside all doubt of the reference to the fourth Gospel."—*Das Christenthum Justins des Märtyrers*, Erlangen, 1878.

philosophy, the doctrine of the *incarnation* of the Logos was utterly foreign to that philosophy, and could only have been derived, it would seem, from the Gospel of John.* He accordingly speaks very often in language similar to that of John (i. 14) of the Logos as "made flesh," † or as "having become man." ‡ That in the last phrase he should prefer the term "man" to the Hebraistic "flesh" can excite no surprise. With reference to the deity of the Logos and his instrumental agency in creation, compare also especially *Apol.* ii. 6, "through him God created all things" (*δι' αὐτοῦ πάντα ἔκτισε*), *Dial.* c. 56, and *Apol.* i. 63, with John i. 1–3. Since the Fathers who immediately followed Justin, as Theophilus, Irenæus, Clement, Tertullian, unquestionably founded their doctrine of the incarnation of the Logos on the Gospel of John, the presumption is that Justin did the same. He professes to hold his view, in which he owns that some Chris-

---

p. 350. Weizsäcker is equally strong.—*Untersuchungen über die evang. Geschichte*, Gotha, 1864, pp. 228, 229.

Dr. Edwin A. Abbott, in the very interesting article *Gospels* in vol. x. of the ninth edition of the Encyclopædia Britannica, objects that Justin cannot have quoted the Fourth Gospel here, because "he is arguing for baptism by *water*," and "it is inconceivable that . . . he should not only quote inaccurately, but omit the very words [John iii. 5] that were best adapted to support his argument." (p. 821.) But Justin is not addressing an "argument" to the Roman Emperor and Senate for the necessity of baptism by water, but simply giving an account of Christian rites and Christian worship. And it is not the mere rite of baptism by water as such, but the necessity of the new birth through repentance and a voluntary change of life on the part of him who dedicates himself to God by this rite, on which Justin lays the main stress,—"the baptism of the soul from wrath and covetousness, envy and hatred." (Comp. *Dial.* cc. 13, 14, 18.) Moreover, the simple word ἀναγεννηθῆτε, as he uses it in the immediate context, and as it was often used, includes the idea of baptism. This fact alone answers the objection. A perusal of the chapter in which Justin treats the subject (*Apol.* i. 61) will show that it was not at all necessary to his purpose in quoting the words of Christ to introduce the ἐξ ὕδατος. It would almost seem as if Dr. Abbott must have been thinking of the Clementine Homilies (xi. 24–27; xiii. 21), where excessive importance *is* attached to the mere element of water.

* See Delitzsch, *Messianic Prophecies* (Edin. 1880), p. 115. See Philo, *De Prof.* c. 19, prol. i. p. 561, ed. M.

† σαρκοποιηθείς; *e.g.*, *Apol.* c. 32, ὁ λόγος, ὃς τίνα τρόπον σαρκοποιηθεὶς ἄνθρωπος γέγονεν. So c. 66 *bis*; *Dial.* cc. 45, 84, 87, 100. Comp. *Dial.* cc. 48 ("was born a man of like nature with us, having flesh"), 70 ("became embodied").

‡ ἄνθρωπος γενόμενος; *Apol.* i. cc. 5 ("the Logos himself who took form and became man"), 23 *bis*, 32, 42, 50, 53, 63 *bis*; *Apol.* ii. c. 13; *Dial.* cc. 48, 57, 64, 67, 68 *bis*, 76, 85, 100, 101, 125 *bis*. I have availed myself in this and the preceding note of the references given by Professor Drummond in his article "Justin Martyr and the Fourth Gospel," in the *Theol. Review* for April and July, 1877; see vol. xiv., p. 172. To this valuable essay I am much indebted, and shall have occasion to refer to it repeatedly. Professor Drummond compares at length Justin's doctrine of the Logos with that of the proem to the Fourth Gospel, and decides rightly, I think, that the statement of the former "is, beyond all question, in a more developed form" than that of the latter. In John it is important to observe that λόγος is used with a meaning derived from the sense of "word" rather than "reason," as in Philo and Justin. The subject is too large to be entered upon here.

tians do not agree with him, "because we have been commanded by Christ himself not to follow the doctrines of men, but those which were proclaimed by the blessed prophets and *taught by* HIM." (*Dial.* c. 48.) Now, as Canon Westcott observes, "the Synoptists do not anywhere declare Christ's pre-existence." * And where could Justin suppose himself to have found this doctrine taught by Christ except in the Fourth Gospel? Compare *Apol.* i. 46: "That Christ is the first-born of God, being the Logos [the divine Reason] of which every race of men have been partakers [comp. John i. 4, 5, 9], we *have been taught* and have declared before. And those who have lived according to Reason are Christians, even though they were deemed atheists; as, for example, Socrates and Heraclitus and those like them among the Greeks."

(*b*) But more may be said. In one place (*Dial.* c. 105) Justin, according to the natural construction of his language and the course of his argument, appears to refer to the "Memoirs" as the source from which he and other Christians had learnt that Christ as the Logos was the "only-begotten" Son of God, a title applied to him by John alone among the New Testament writers; see John i. 14, 18; iii. 16, 18. The passage reads, "For that he was the only-begotten of the Father of the universe, having been begotten by him in a peculiar manner as his Logos and Power, and having afterwards become man through the virgin, as we have learned from the Memoirs, I showed before." It is *possible* that the clause, "as we have learned from the Memoirs," refers not to the main proposition of the sentence, but only to the fact of the birth from a virgin; but the context as well as the natural construction leads to a different view, as Professor Drummond has ably shown in the article in the *Theological Review* (xiv. 178–182) already referred to in a note. He observes: —

"The passage is part of a very long comparison, which Justin institutes between the twenty-second Psalm and the recorded events of

* "Introd. to the Gospel of St. John," in *The Holy Bible . . . with . . . Commentary*, etc., ed. by F. C. Cook, *N.T.* vol. ii. (1880), p. lxxxiv.

Christ's life. For the purposes of this comparison he refers to or quotes "the Gospel" once, and "the Memoirs" ten times, and further refers to the latter three times in the observations which immediately follow. . . . They are appealed to here because they furnish the successive steps of the proof by which the Psalm is shown to be prophetic."

In this case the words in the Psalm (xxii. 20, 21) which have to be illustrated are, "Deliver my soul from the sword, and my only-begotten [Justin perhaps read "*thy* only-begotten"] from the power of the dog. Save me from the mouth of the lion, and my humiliation from the horns of unicorns." "These words," Justin remarks, "are again in a similar manner a teaching and prophecy of the things that belonged to him [τῶν ὄντων αὐτῷ] and that were going to happen. For that he was the only-begotten," etc., as quoted above. Professor Drummond well observes: —

"There is here no ground of comparison whatever except in the word μονογενής ["only-begotten"]. . . . It is evident that Justin understood this as referring to Christ; and accordingly he places the same word emphatically at the beginning of the sentence in which he proves the reference of this part of the Psalm to Jesus. For the same reason he refers not only to events, but to τὰ ὄντα αὐτῷ ["the things that belonged to him"]. These are taken up first in the nature and title of μονογενής, which immediately suggests λόγος and δύναμις ["Logos" and "power"], while the events are introduced and discussed afterwards. The allusion here to the birth through the virgin has nothing to do with the quotation from the Old Testament, and is probably introduced simply to show how Christ, although the only-begotten Logos, was nevertheless a man. If the argument were, — These words allude to Christ, because the Memoirs tell us that he was born from a virgin, — it would be utterly incoherent. If it were, — These words allude to Christ, because the Memoirs say that he was the only-begotten, — it would be perfectly valid from Justin's point of view. It would not, however, be suitable for a Jew, for whom the fact that Christ was μονογενής, not being an historical event, had to rest upon other authority; and therefore Justin changing his usual form, says that he had already explained to him a doctrine which the Christians learned from the Memoirs. It appears to me, then, most probable, that the peculiar Johannine title μονογενής existed in the Gospels used by Justin.*

In what follows, Prof. Drummond answers Thoma's ob-

* Justin also designates Christ as "the only-begotten Son" in a fragment of his work against Marcion, preserved by Irenæus, *Hær.* iv. 6. § 2. Comp. Justin, *Apol.* i. c. 23; ii. c. 6; *Dial.* c. 48.

jections * to this view of the passage, correcting some mistranslations. In the expression, "as I showed before," the reference may be, not to c. 100, but to c. 61 and similar passages, where it is argued that the Logos was "begotten by God before all creatures," which implies a unique generation.

(*c*) In the Dialogue with Trypho (c. 88), Justin cites as the words of John the Baptist: "I am not the Christ, but the voice of one crying"; οὐκ εἰμὶ ὁ Χριστός, ἀλλὰ φωνὴ βοῶντος. This declaration, "I am not the Christ," and this application to himself of the language of Isaiah, are attributed to the Baptist only in the Gospel of John (i. 20, 23; comp. iii. 28). Hilgenfeld recognizes here the use of this Gospel.

(*d*) Justin says of the Jews, "They are justly upbraided . . . by Christ himself as knowing neither the Father nor the Son" (*Apol.* i. 63). Comp. John viii. 19, "Ye neither know me nor my Father"; and xvi. 3, "They have not known the Father nor me." It is true that Justin quotes in this connection Matt. xi. 27; but his language seems to be influenced by the passages in John above cited, in which alone the Jews are directly addressed.

(*e*) Justin says that "Christ healed those who were blind from their birth," τοὺς ἐκ γενετῆς πηρούς (*Dial.* c. 49; comp. *Apol.* i. 22, ἐκ γενετῆς πονηρούς, where several editors, though not Otto, would substitute πηρούς by conjecture). There seems to be a reference here to John ix. 1, where we have τυφλὸν ἐκ γενετῆς, the phrase ἐκ γενετῆς, "from birth," being peculiar to John among the Evangelists, and πηρός being a common synonyme of τυφλός; comp. the Apostolical Constitutions v. 7. § 17, where we have ὁ ἐκ γενετῆς πηρός in a clear reference

* In Hilgenfeld's *Zeitschrift für wiss. Theol.*, 1875, xviii. 551 ff. For other discussions of this passage, one may see Semisch, *Die apost. Denkwürdigkeiten* u.s.w., p. 188 f.: Hilgenfeld, *Krit. Untersuchungen* u.s.w., p. 300 f. (*versus* Semisch); Riggenbach, *Die Zeugnisse f. d. Ev. Johannis*, Basel, 1866, p. 163 f.; Tischendorf, *Wann wurden unsere Evangelien verfasst?* p. 32, 4e Aufl. But Professor Drummond's treatment of the question is the most thorough.

Grimm (*Theol. Stud. u. Krit.*, 1851, p. 687 ff.) agrees with Semisch that it is "in the highest degree arbitrary" to refer Justin's expression, "as we have learned from the Memoirs," merely to the participial clause which mentions the birth from a virgin; but like Thoma, who agrees with him that the reference is to the designation "only-begotten," he thinks that Justin has in mind merely the confession of Peter (Matt. xvi. 16), referred to in *Dial.* c. 100. This rests on the false assumption that Justin can only be referring back to c. 100, and makes him argue that "the Son" merely is equivalent to "the only-begotten Son" to this passage of John, and the Clementine Homilies xix. 22, where περὶ τοῦ ἐκ γενετῆς πηροῦ occurs also in a similar reference.* John is the only Evangelist who mentions the healing of any congenital infirmity.

(*f*) The exact coincidence between Justin (*Apol.* i. 52; comp. *Dial.* cc. 14 (quoted as from *Hosea*), 32, 64, 118) and John (xix. 37) in citing Zechariah xii. 10 in a form different from the Septuagint, ὄψονται εἰς ὃν ἐξεκέντησαν, "they shall look on him whom they pierced," instead of ἐπιβλέψονται πρός με ἀνθ' ὧν κατωρχήσαντο, is remarkable, and not sufficiently explained by supposing both to have borrowed from Rev. i. 7, "every eye shall see him, and they who pierced him." Much stress has been laid on this coincidence by Semisch (p. 200 ff.) and Tischendorf (p. 34); but it is possible, if not rather probable, that Justin and John have independently followed a reading of the Septuagint which had already attained currency in the first century as a correction of the text in conformity with the Hebrew.†

(*g*) Compare *Apol.* i. 13 (cited by Prof. Drummond, p. 323), "Jesus Christ who became our teacher of these things and *was born to this end* (εἰς τοῦτο γεννηθέντα), who was crucified under Pontius Pilate," with Christ's answer to Pilate (John xviii. 37), "To this end have I been born, εἰς τοῦτο γεγέννημαι, . . . that I might bear witness to the truth."

(*h*) Justin says (*Dial.* c. 56, p. 276 D), "I affirm that he never did or spake any thing but what he that made the world, above whom there is no other God, willed that he should both do and speak"; ‡ comp. John viii. 28, 29: "As

---

*The context in Justin, as Otto justly remarks, proves that πηρούς must here signify "blind," not "maimed"; comp. the quotation from Isa. xxxv. 5, which precedes, and the "causing this one to see," which follows. Keim's exclamation — "not a blind man at all!" — would have been spared, if he had attended to this. (See his *Gesch. Jesu von Nazara*, i. 139, note; i. 189, Eng. trans.)

† See Credner, *Beiträge* u.s.w., ii. 293 ff. See further on this quotation, p. 66, *infra*.

‡ Dr. Davidson (*Introd. to the Study of the N.T.*, London, 1868, ii. 376) translates the last clause, "intended that he should do and *to associate with*" (sic). Though the meaning "to converse with," and then "to speak," "to say," is not assigned to ὁμιλεῖν in Liddell and Scott, or Rost and Palm's edition of Passow, Justin in the very next sentence uses λαλεῖν as an equivalent substitute, and this meaning is common in the later Greek. See Sophocles, *Greek Lex.* s.v. ὁμιλέω. Of Dr. Davidson's translation I must confess my inability to make either grammar or sense.

the Father taught me, I speak these things; and . . . I always do the things that please him"; also John iv. 34; v. 19, 30; vii. 16; xii. 49, 50. In the language of Trypho which immediately follows (p. 277 A), "We do not suppose that you represent him to have *said* or done or *spoken* anything contrary to the will of the Creator of the universe," we are particularly reminded of John xii. 49, — "The Father who sent me hath himself given me a commandment, what I should *say* and what I should *speak*."

(*i*) Referring to a passage of the Old Testament as signifying that Christ "was to rise from the dead on the third day after his crucifixion," Justin subjoins (*Dial.* c. 100), "which he received from his Father," or more literally, "which [thing] he has, having received it from his Father," ὃ ἀπὸ τοῦ πατρὸς λαβὼν ἔχει. A reference here to John x. 18 seems probable, where Jesus says respecting his life, "I have authority (ἐξουσίαν) to lay it down, and I have authority to receive it again (πάλιν λαβεῖν αὐτήν); this charge I received from my Father" (ἔλαβον παρὰ τοῦ πατρός μου).

(*k*) Justin says, "We were taught that the bread and wine were the flesh and blood of that Jesus who was made flesh." (*Apol.* i. c. 66.) This use of the term "flesh" instead of "body" in describing the bread of the Eucharist suggests John vi. 51–56.

(*l*) Professor Drummond notes that Justin, like John (iii. 14, 15), regards the elevation of the brazen serpent in the wilderness as typical of the crucifixion (*Apol.* i. c. 60; *Dial.* cc. 91, 94, 131), and in speaking of it says that it denoted "salvation to those who flee for refuge to him who sent his crucified Son into the world" (*Dial.* c. 91).* "Now this idea of God's sending his Son into the world occurs in the same connection in John iii. 17, and strange as it may appear, it is an idea which in the New Testament is peculiar to John." Prof. Drummond further observes that "in the four instances in which John speaks of Christ as being sent into the world, he prefers ἀποστέλλω, so that Justin's phrase is

* Or, as it is expressed in *Dial.* c. 94, "salvation to those *who believe in him* who was to die through this sign, the cross," which comes nearer to John iii. 15.

not entirely coincident with the Johannine. But the use of πέμπω ["to send"] itself is curious. Except by John, it is applied to Christ in the New Testament only twice, whereas John uses it [thus] twenty-five times. Justin's language, therefore, in the thought which it expresses, in the selection of words, and in its connection, is closely related to John's, and has no other parallel in the New Testament." (*Theol. Rev.* xiv. 324.) Compare also *Dial.* c. 140, "according to the will of the Father who sent him," etc., and *Dial.* c. 17, "the only blameless and righteous Light sent from God to men." (Prof. Drummond seems to have overlooked Gal. iv. 4.)

(*m*) Lücke, Otto, Semisch, Keim, Mangold, and Drummond are disposed to find a reminiscence of John i. 13 in Justin's language where, after quoting from Genesis xlix. 11, he says, "since his blood was not begotten of human seed, but by the will of God" (*Dial.* c. 63; comp. the similar language *Apol.* i. 32; *Dial.* cc. 54, "by the power of God"; 76). They suppose that Justin referred John i. 13 to Christ, following an early reading of the passage, namely, ὅς . . . ἐγεννήθη, "who *was* born" [*or* "begotten"] instead of "who *were* born." We find this reading in Irenæus (*Hær.* iii. 16. § 2; 19. § 2), Tertullian (*De Carne Christi* cc. 19, 24), Ambrose once, Augustine once, also in Codex Veronensis (b) of the Old Latin, and some other authorities. Tertullian indeed boldly charges the Valentinians with corrupting the text by changing the singular to the plural. Rönsch, whom no one will call an "apologist," remarks, "The citation of these words . . . certainly belongs to the proofs that Justin Martyr knew the Gospel of John." * I have noticed this, in deference to these authorities, but am not confident that there is any reference in Justin's language to John i. 13.

(*n*) Justin says (*Dial.* c. 88), "The *Apostles* have written" that at the baptism of Jesus "as he came up from the water the Holy Spirit as a dove lighted upon him." The descent of the Holy Spirit as a dove is mentioned by the Apostles Matthew and John (Matt. iii. 16; John i. 32, 33). This is

* *Das neue Testament Tertullians*, Leipz. 1871, p. 654.

the only place in which Justin uses the expression "the Apostles have written."

(*o*) Justin says (*Dial.* c. 103) that Pilate sent Jesus to Herod *bound*. The binding is not mentioned by Luke; but if Justin used the Gospel of John, the mistake is easily explained through a confusion in memory of Luke xxiii. 7 with John xviii. 24 (comp. ver. 12); and this seems the most natural explanation; see however Matt. xxvii. 2; Mark xv. 1. Examples of such a confusion of different passages repeatedly occur in Justin's quotations from the Old Testament, as also of his citing the Old Testament for facts which it does not contain.*

(*p*) The remark of Justin that the Jews dared to call Jesus a magician (comp. Matt. ix. 34; xii. 24) and *a deceiver of the people* (λαόπλανον) reminds one strongly of John vii. 12; see however also Matt. xxvii. 63.—"Through his stripes," says Justin (*Dial.* c. 17), "there is healing to those who through him come to the Father," which suggests John xiv. 6, "No man cometh to the Father but through me"; but the reference is uncertain; comp. Eph. ii. 18, and Heb. vii. 25 with the similar expression in *Dial.* c. 43.—So also it is not clear that in the προσκυνοῦμεν, λόγῳ καὶ ἀληθείᾳ τιμῶντες (*Apol.* i. 6) there is any allusion to John iv. 24.†—I pass over sundry passages where Bindemann, Otto, Semisch, Thoma, Drummond and others have found resemblances more or less striking between the language of Justin and

* See, for example, *Apol.* i. 44, where the words in Deut. xxx. 15, 19, are represented as addressed to *Adam* (comp. Gen. ii. 16, 17); and *Apol.* i. 60, where Justin refers to Num. xxi. 8, 9 for various particulars found only in his own imagination. The extraordinary looseness with which he quotes Plato here (as elsewhere) may also be noted (see the *Timæus* c. 12, p. 36 B, C). On Justin's quotations from the Old Testament, which are largely marked by the same characteristics as his quotations from the Gospels, see Credner, *Beiträge* u.s.w., vol. ii. (1838); Norton, *Genuineness* etc., i. 213 ff., and Addit. Notes, p. ccxviii. ff., 2d ed., 1846 (1st ed. 1837); Semisch, *Die apost. Denkwürdigkeiten* u.s.w. (1848), p. 239 ff.; Hilgenfeld, *Krit. Untersuchungen* (1850), p. 46 ff.; Westcott, *Canon*, p. 121 ff., 172 ff., 4th ed. (1875); Sanday, *The Gospels in the Second Century* (1876), pp. 40 ff., 111 ff.

† Grimm, however, finds here "an unmistakable reminiscence" of John iv. 24. He thinks Justin used λόγῳ for πνεύματι and τιμῶντες for προσκυνοῦντες because πνεῦμα and προσκυνοῦμεν immediately precede. (*Theol. Stud. u. Krit.*, 1851, p. 691.) But λόγῳ καὶ ἀληθείᾳ seem to mean simply, "in accordance with reason and truth"; comp. *Apol.* i. 68, cited by Otto, also c. 13, μετὰ λόγου τιμῶμεν.

John, leaving them to the not very tender mercies of Zeller * and Hilgenfeld. †

(*q*) Justin's vindication of Christians for not keeping the Jewish Sabbath on the ground that "God has carried on the same administration of the universe during that day as during all others" (*Dial.* c. 29, comp. c. 23) is, as Mr. Norton observes, "a thought so remarkable, that there can be little doubt that he borrowed it from what was said by our Saviour when the Jews were enraged at his having performed a miracle on the Sabbath:—'My Father has been working hitherto as I am working.'"—His argument also against the observance of the Jewish Sabbath from the fact that circumcision was permitted on that day may (*Dial.* c. 27) have been borrowed from John vii. 22, 23.

(*r*) I will notice particularly only one more passage, in which Professor Drummond proposes an original and very plausible explanation of a difficulty. In the larger Apology (c. 35), as he observes, the following words are quoted from Isaiah (lviii. 2), αἰτοῦσι με νῦν κρίσιν, "they now ask of me judgment"; and in evidence that this prophecy was fulfilled in Christ, Justin asserts, "they mocked him, and set him on the judgment-seat (ἐκάθισαν ἐπὶ βήματος), and said, Judge for us." This proceeding is nowhere recorded in our Gospels, but in John xix. 13 we read, "Pilate therefore brought Jesus out, and sat on the judgment-seat" (καὶ ἐκάθισεν ἐπὶ βήματος). But the words just quoted in the Greek, the correspondence of which with those of Justin will be noticed, admit in themselves the rendering, "and *set him* on the judgment-seat"; ‡ and what was more natural, as Prof. Drummond remarks, than that Justin, in his eagerness to find a fulfilment of the prophecy, should take them in this sense? "He might then add the statement that the people said κρῖνον ἡμῖν ['judge for us'] as an obvious inference from the fact of Christ's having been placed on the tribunal, just as in an earlier chapter (c. 32) he appends to the synoptic account the circum-

* *Die äusseren Zeugnisse . . . des vierten Evang.*, in the *Theol. Jahrbücher* (Tübingen) 1845, p. 600 ff.

† *Kritische Untersuchungen* u.s.w., p. 302 f.

‡ Dr. Hort has pointed out to me that Justin uses the word transitively in *Dial.* 32, καθίζοντα αὐτὸν ἐν δεξιᾷ αὐτοῦ, comp. Eph. i. 20, though in the New Testament it is commonly intransitive. See also its use with reference to *judges* I. Cor. vi. 4.

stance that the ass on which Christ rode into Jerusalem was bound to a vine, in order to bring the event into connection with Genesis xlix. 11." (*Theol. Review*, xiv. 328.)

These evidences of Justin's use of the Gospel of John are strengthened somewhat by an indication, which has been generally overlooked, of his use of the First Epistle of John. In 1 John iii. 1 we read, according to the text now adopted by the best critics, as Lachmann, Tischendorf, Tregelles, Alford, Westcott and Hort, "Behold what love the Father hath bestowed upon us, that we should be called children of God; and we are so"; *ἵνα τέκνα θεοῦ κληθῶμεν, καὶ ἐσμέν.* This addition to the common text, *καὶ ἐσμέν*, "and we are," is supported by a great preponderance of external evidence. Compare now Justin (*Dial.* c. 123): "We are both called true children of God, and we are so"; *καὶ θεοῦ τέκνα ἀληθινὰ καλούμεθα καὶ ἐσμέν.* The coincidence seems too remarkable to be accidental. Hilgenfeld takes the same view (*Einleit. in d. N. T.*, p. 69), and so Ewald (*Die johan. Schriften*, ii. 395, Anm. 4).

It also deserves to be considered that, as Justin wrote a work "Against all Heresies" (*Apol.* i. 26), among which he certainly included those of Valentinus and Basilides (*Dial.* c. 35; cf. Tertull. *Adv. Valentinianos*, c. 5), he could hardly have been ignorant of a book which, according to Irenæus, the Valentinians used *plenissime*, and to which the Basilidians and apparently Basilides himself also appealed (Hippol. *Ref. Hær.* vii. 22, 27). Credner recognizes the weight of this argument.* It can only be met by maintaining what is altogether improbable, that merely the *later* Valentinians and Basilidians made use of the Gospel,—a point which we shall examine hereafter.

In judging of the indications of Justin's use of the Fourth Gospel, the passages cited in addition to those which relate to his Logos doctrine will strike different persons differently. There will be few, however, I think, who will not feel that the one first discussed (that relating to the new birth) is in itself almost a decisive proof of such a use, and that the one relating to John the Baptist (*c*) is also strong. In regard to

* *Geschichte des neutest. Kanon* (1860), p. 15 f.; comp. pp. 9, 12.

not a few others, while the *possibility* of accidental agreement must be conceded, the probability is decidedly against this, and the accumulated probabilities form an argument of no little weight. It is not then, I believe, too much to say, that the strong presumption from the universal reception of our four Gospels as sacred books in the time of Irenæus that Justin's "Memoirs of Christ composed by Apostles and their companions" were the same books, is decidedly confirmed by these evidences of his use of the Fourth Gospel. We will next consider the further confirmation of this fact afforded by writers who flourished between the time of Justin and Irenæus, and then notice some objections to the view which has been presented.

The most weighty testimony is that of Tatian, the Assyrian, a disciple of Justin. His literary activity may be placed at about A.D. 155–170 (Lightfoot). In his "Address to the Greeks" he repeatedly quotes the Fourth Gospel, though without naming the author, in one case using the expression (τὸ εἰρημένον) which is several times employed in the New Testament (*e.g.* Acts ii. 16; Rom. iv. 18) in introducing a quotation from the Scriptures; see his *Orat. ad Græc.* c. 13, "And this then is that which hath been said, The darkness comprehendeth [*or* overcometh] not the light" (John i. 5); see also c. 19 (John i. 3); c. 4 (John iv. 24).* Still more important is the fact that he composed a Harmony of our Four Gospels which he called the *Diatessaron* (*i.e.* "the Gospel made out of Four"). This fact is attested by Eusebius (*Hist. Eccl.* iv. 29),† Epiphanius (*Hær.* xlvi. 1), who, however, writes from hearsay, and Theodoret, who in his work on Heresies (*Hær. Fab.* i. 20) says that he found more than two hundred copies of the book held in esteem in his diocese, and substituted for it copies of our Four Gospels.

* Even Zeller does not dispute that Tatian quotes the Fourth Gospel, and ascribed it to the Apostle John. (*Theol. Jahrb.* 1847, p. 158.) Cf. Volkmar, *Ursprung*, u.s.w., p. 35.

† An expression used by Eusebius (οὐκ οἶδ' ὅπως, literally, "I know not how") has been misunderstood by many as implying that he had not seen the work; but Lightfoot has shown conclusively that this inference is wholly unwarranted. It only implies that the plan of the work seemed strange to him. See *Contemporary Review* for May, 1877, p. 1136, where Lightfoot cites 26 examples of this use of the phrase from the work of Origen against Celsus.

He tells us that Tatian, who is supposed to have prepared the Harmony after he became a Gnostic Encratite, had "cut away the genealogies and such other passages as show the Lord to have been born of the seed of David after the flesh." But notwithstanding this mutilation, the work seems to have been very popular in the orthodox churches of Syria as a convenient compendium. The celebrated Syrian Father, Ephraem, the deacon of Edessa, who died A.D. 373, wrote a commentary on it, according to Dionysius Bar-Salibi, who flourished in the last part of the twelfth century. Bar-Salibi was well acquainted with the work, citing it in his own Commentary on the Gospels, and distinguishing it from the Diatessaron of Ammonius, and from a later work by Elias Salamensis, also called Aphthonius. He mentions that it began with John i. 1 — "In the beginning was the Word." (See Assemani, *Biblioth. Orient.* ii. 158 ff.) Besides Ephraem, Aphraates, an earlier Syrian Father (A.D. 337) appears to have used it (*Hom.* i. p. 13 ed. Wright); and in the *Doctrine of Addai*, an apocryphal Syriac work, written probably not far from the middle of the third century, which purports to give an account of the early history of Christianity at Edessa, the people are represented as coming together "to the prayers of the service, and to [the reading of] the Old Testament and the New of the Diatessaron." * The *Doctrine of Addai* does not name the author of the *Diatessaron* thus read; but the facts already mentioned make the presumption strong that it was Tatian's. A scholion on Cod. 72 of the Gospels cites "Tatian's Gospel" for a remarkable reading of Matt. xxvii. 49 found in many ancient MSS.; and

---

* In Cureton's *Ancient Syriac Documents* (Lond. 1864) the text, published from a MS. in the British Museum, is here corrupt, reading *Ditonron*, a word without meaning; comp. Pratten's *Syriac Documents* (1871), p. 25, note, in the Ante-Nicene Christian Library, vol. xx. Cureton conjectured that the true reading was *Diatessaron* (see his note, p. 158), and his conjecture is confirmed by the St. Petersburg MS. published by Dr. George Phillips, *The Doctrine of Addai*, London, 1876; see his note, p. 34 f. Cureton's Syriac text (p. 15), as well as his translation (p. 15), reads *Ditonron*, not *Ditornon*, as Lightfoot, Pratten, and Phillips erroneously state, being misled by a misprint in Cureton's note. Phillips gives the reading correctly in the note to his Syriac text (p. 36). Moesinger, in the work described below, is also misled, spelling the word *Diathurnun* (Præf. p. iv). The difference between *Ditonron* and *Diatessaron* in the Syriac is very slight, affecting only a single letter.

it is also cited for a peculiar reading of Luke vii. 42.* So far the evidence is clear, consistent, and conclusive; but on the ground of a confusion between Tatian's Harmony and that of Ammonius on the part of a Syrian writer of the thirteenth century (Gregorius Abulpharagius or Bar-Hebræus), and of the two *persons* by a still later writer, Ebed-Jesu, both of which confusions can be traced to a misunderstanding of the language of Bar-Salibi, and for other reasons equally weak, † the fact that Tatian's work was a Harmony of our Four Gospels has been questioned by some German critics, and of course by *Supernatural Religion.* But the whole subject has been so thoroughly discussed and its obscurities so well cleared up by Bishop Lightfoot, in an article in the *Contemporary Review* for May, 1877, that the question may be regarded as settled. ‡ Lightfoot's view is confirmed by the recent publication of Ephraem's Commentary on the

---

* See Tischendorf, *N.T. Gr.* ed. 8va, on Matt. xxvii. 49, and Scholz, *N.T. Gr.*, vol. i, p. cxiix., and p. 243, note *x*.

† Such as that Victor of Capua (A.D. 545) says that it was called *Diapente* (*i.e.*, "made out of five"). But this is clearly a slip of the pen of Victor himself, or a mistake of some scribe; for, as Hilgenfeld (*Einleit.* p. 79, note) and Lightfoot remark, Victor is simply reporting *Eusebius's* account of it, and not only does Eusebius say that Tatian called it the *Diatessaron*, but Victor himself has just described it as "*unum ex quatuor.*" The strange mistake, for it can be nothing else, may possibly be accounted for by the fact that *Diatessaron* and *Diapente* being both musical terms (cf. Plut. *Quæst. Conviv.* iii. 9, § 1; *De Mus.* cc. 22, 23; Macrob. in *Somn. Scip.* i. 6, §§ 43, 44; ii. 1, §§ 15–25; Vitruv. v. 4, §§ 7, 8; Martian. Capella, ix., §§ 950 ff; Censorinus, x. 6; Philo, *De Opif. Mundi*, c. 15, and Müller's note, p. 214 ff), one might naturally recall the other, and lead to an unconscious substitution on the part of the author or of some absent-minded copyist. Such slips of the pen, or *heterographies*, are not uncommon. To take examples from two books which I have just been using: Zacagni, *Collectanea Mon. Vet.* p. 536, note 5, says "Anno Christi *quingentesimo* quinquagesimo octavo" when he means "*quadringentesimo*"; Charteris, *Canonicity* (Edin. 1880), p. xlv., note, no. 4, says "Eusebius" for "Papias," and, in quoting Lardner (*ibid.* p. 42, note 1, end), substitutes "*New* Testament" for "*Old* Testament". Under no circumstances can any inference about the composition of the work be drawn from this *Diapente*, for Victor derives his information from Eusebius, and not only do all the Greek MSS. in the passage referred to read *Diatessaron*, but this reading is confirmed by the very ancient, probably contemporary, Syriac version of Eusebius, preserved in a MS. of the sixth century, and by the Latin version of Rufinus, made a century and a half before Victor wrote. (See Lightfoot, p. 1143.) The mistake ascribed to the Syriac lexicographer Bar-Bahlul is proved to be due to an interpolator. (See Lightfoot, p. 1139, note.) The statement of Epiphanius, the most untrustworthy and blundering of the Fathers, that "it is called by some the Gospel according to the Hebrews" (*Hær.* xlvi. 1), if it had any foundation beyond a mere guess of the writer, may have originated from the omission of the genealogies, which were omitted also in one form of the Gospel according to the Hebrews (Epiph. *Hær.* xxx. 13, 14). The supposition that it *was* that Gospel contradicts all our information about the two works except the circumstance just mentioned; and that it had *additions* from that Gospel is a conjecture for which we have not a particle of evidence. (See Lightfoot, p. 1141; Lipsius in Smith and Wace's *Dict. of Christian Biog.* ii. 714.)

‡ To Lightfoot's article I am much indebted. The other writers who treat of the subject most fully are Credner, *Beiträge*, u.s.w., i. 437–451, who has thrown more darkness upon it than anybody else; Daniel, *Tatianus der Apologet* (Halle, 1837), pp. 87–111, who has refuted Credner's arguments; Semisch, *Tatiani Diatessaron*, Vratisl. 1856; Hilgenfeld, *Einleit. in d. N.T.* (1875), pp. 75–79; *Supernatural Religion*, vol. ii., pp. 148–159, 7th ed.; and E. B. Nicholson, *The Gospel according to the Hebrews* (London, 1879), p. 16 f., and pp. 126–133, who does not appear to have seen Lightfoot's article, but exposes independently many of the errors and fallacies of *Supernatural Religion*. See also Norton, *Genuineness of the Gospels*, iii. 292 ff.

Diatessaron, to which I have already had occasion to refer.* This exists only in an Armenian version of the Syriac, made, it is supposed, in the fifth century. The Armenian text was published in the second volume of the collected Works of St. Ephraem in Armenian, printed at Venice in 1836 (4 vols. 8vo); but Aucher's Latin translation of the Commentary, revised and edited by G. Moesinger, who compared it with another Armenian manuscript, first appeared at Venice in 1876, and the work has hitherto been almost unnoticed by scholars.† It should be observed that Ephraem's commentary is only on select passages of the Harmony, unless the work which has come down to us is merely an abridgment. But there seems to be no ground for questioning the genuineness of the work ascribed to Ephraem; and little or no ground for doubting that the Harmony on which he is commenting is Tatian's, in accordance with the account of Dionysius Bar-Salibi.‡ It agrees with what we know of Tatian's in omitting the genealogies and in beginning with the first verse of the Gospel of John. Further, the character of the text, so far as we can judge of it from a translation of a translation, is such as to lend confirmation to the view that it is Tatian's. It presents some very ancient various readings which accord remarkably with those of Justin Martyr and other early writers, and with the Curetonian Syriac where it differs from the later Peshito.‖

---

* See Note A, no. 4.

† The volume is entitled: *Evangelii concordantis Expositio facta a Sancto Ephraemo Doctore Syro. In Latinum translata a R. P. Joanne Baptista Aucher Mechitarista cujus Versionem emendavit, Adnotationibus illustravit et edidit Dr. Georgius Moesinger.* Venetiis, Libraria PP. Mechitaristarum in Monasterio S. Lazari. 1876. 8vo. pp. xii., 292. Lipsius, art. *Gospels, Apocryphal*, in Smith and Wace's *Dict. of Christian Biog.*, vol. ii. (London, 1880), p. 713, is not even aware that the Armenian translation has been published.

‡ See Moesinger, *ubi supra*, Præf. p. ii. ff.

‖ We find, for example, the very ancient punctuation or construction which ends the sentence in John i. 3 with οὐδὲ ἕν, "not even one thing," connecting ὃ γέγονεν with ver. 4. (See Moesinger's edition, p. 5.) This accords with the citation of the passage by Tatian (*Orat. ad Græc.* c. 19). In Matt. i. 25, we read "sancte (*or* in sanctitate) habitabat cum ea" (Moesinger, pp. 23, 25, 26); so the Curetonian Syriac. In Matt. viii. 10 (p. 74), it reads, "*Non in aliquo* in Israël tantam fidem inveni," with Cod. Vaticanus (B), several of the best cursives, the MSS. a g^1. k q of the Old Latin, the Curetonian Syriac, Sahidic, Coptic, and Æthiopic versions, the Harclean Syriac in the margin, Augustine once, and the "*Opus Imperfectum*" on Matt. In Matt. xi. 27 (Moesinger, pp. 117, 216), it agrees with Justin, the Clementine Homilies, and the Gnostics in Irenæus, in the transposition of the clauses relating to the Father and the Son. (See

We may regard it then, I conceive, as an established fact that Tatian's *Diatessaron* was a Harmony of our four Gospels. So difficult and laborious a work would hardly have been undertaken, except to meet a want which had been widely felt. It implies that the four books used were recognized by those for whom it was intended as authoritative, and as possessing equal authority. Can we then believe that Tatian's Harmony represented a different set of books from the "Memoirs called Gospels" of his master Justin, which were read at the meetings for public worship in churches all over the Christian world as the authentic records of the life and teaching of Christ, the production of Apostles and their companions? Does not Tatian's unquestionable use of the Gospel of John in particular confirm the strong presumption from other facts that this Gospel was included in the "Memoirs" used by his master and by Christians generally twenty years before?

This presumption receives further confirmation from other testimonies to the existence and use of the Fourth Gospel between the time of Justin Martyr and Irenæus.

The treatise or fragment *On the Resurrection*, which Otto with many others ascribes to Justin, if not genuine, probably belongs to this period. In c. 1 we read, "The Logos of God, who was [*or* became] his Son, came to us clothed in flesh, revealing both himself and the Father, giving to us in himself the resurrection from the dead and the eternal life which follows." The allusions here to John i. 1, 14; xiv. 9; xi. 25, 26, seem unmistakable. So in c. 9, "He permitted them to handle him, and showed in his hands the marks of the nails," we have a reference to John xx. 25, 27, as well as to Luke xxiv. 39.

Melito, bishop of Sardis (*cir.* A.D. 165), in a fragment from

---

Note A, under no. 4.) In Matt. xix. 17, the text is given in Ephraem's commentary in different forms, but it seems to be, substantially, "Unus tantum est bonus, Pater (*or* Deus Pater) qui in cælis" (Moesinger, pp. 169, 170, 173); similarly, Justin Martyr once (*Dial.* c. 101), the Naassenes in Hippolytus (*Adv. Hær.* v. 7, p. 102), the Marcosians in Irenæus (*Hær.* i. 20. § 2), and the Clementine Homilies (xviii. 1, 3); see, for the numerous variations of reading here, Tischendorf's *N.T. Gr.* ed. 8va, *in loc.* Notice also the reading of John vii. 8 ("*Non* ascendo," Moesinger, p. 167); John iii. 13, quoted without the last clause of *text. recept.* (pp. 187, 189, comp. 168); John x. 8 (*ante me*, p. 200); Luke xxii. 44 ("et factus est sudor ejus ut guttæ sanguinis," p. 235; comp. Justin, *Dial.* c. 103).

his work on the Incarnation preserved by Anastasius Sinaita, speaks of Christ as "giving proof to us of his deity by signs [wrought] in the three years after his baptism, and of his humanity in the thirty years before his baptism." * This assignment of a duration of three years to his ministry must have been founded on the Gospel of John, which mentions three Passovers (ii. 13; vi. 4; xi. 55) besides the "feast of the Jews" referred to in John v. 1.

Claudius Apollinaris, bishop of Hierapolis in Phrygia (*cir.* A.D. 166), in a treatise on the Paschal Festival, refers to the apparent difference between John and the Synoptic Gospels as to the time of the death of Jesus. Apollinaris, relying on the Gospel of John, held that it was on the day on which the paschal lamb was killed, the 14th of Nisan; his opponents, appealing to the Gospel of Matthew, maintained that it was on the day following. Both Gospels were evidently received as authoritative by both parties.† He also refers in the same work to the piercing of the side of Jesus and the effusion of water and blood, mentioned only by John (xix. 34).‡

The Epistle of the Churches of Vienne and Lyons in Gaul to those of Asia and Phrygia, giving an account of their persecutions (A.D. 177), quotes the following as the words of the Lord: "There shall come a time in which whosoever killeth you shall think that he is offering a religious service to God," λατρείαν προσφέρειν τῷ θεῷ. The expression in the last clause is the same which is inadequately rendered in the common version "doeth God service" (John xvi. 2).|| The use of the word παράκλητος a little before in the Epistle, "having the

* See Anast. Sinait. *Hodeg.* or *Viæ Dux*, c. 13, in Migne, *Patrol. Gr.* lxxxix. col. 229, or Melito, Frag. vi. in Otto, *Corp. Apol. Christ.*, vol. ix. (1872), p. 416.

† *Chronicon Paschale*, vol. i., pp. 13, 14, ed. Dindorf; Apollinaris in Routh's *Rell. sacræ*, ed. alt. (1846), i. 160; or Otto, *Corp. Apol. Christ.*, ix. 486 f.

‡ *Ibid.* p. 14, ed. Dindorf; Routh, *ibid.* p. 161; Otto, *ubi supra.* For a full view of the evidence of Melito and Apollinaris, and of the considerations which give it weight, see Lightfoot's article, "The Later School of St. John," in the *Contemporary Review* for February, 1876, xxvii. 471 ff.

|| The letter is preserved in large part by Eusebius, *Hist. Eccl.* v. cc. 1-4. It may be consulted conveniently in Routh, *Rell. sacræ*, i. 295 ff., ed. alt. For the quotation, see *Epist.* c. 4; Routh, p. 300; Euseb. v. 1. § 15.

Paraclete within him," also suggests the Gospel of John; comp. John xiv. 16, 17.*

Athenagoras the Athenian (*cir.* A.D. 176), in his *Plea for Christians* addressed to M. Aurelius and Commodus, speaking of "the Logos of God the Father," says that "through him all things were made" (δι' αὐτοῦ πάντα ἐγένετο), the Father and the Son being one; and the Son being in the Father, and the Father in the Son"; language which seems evidently founded on John i. 3; x. 30, 38; xiv. 10, 11; xvii. 21, 22.†

Theophilus, bishop of Antioch A.D. 169–181, in his work in defence of Christianity addressed to Autolycus (A.D. 180), says, "The Holy Scriptures teach us, and all who were moved by the Spirit, among whom John says, 'In the beginning was the word [*or* Logos], and the Word was with God.'" He proceeds to quote John i. 3.‡

The Muratorian Canon (*cir.* A.D. 170), as has already been mentioned, ascribes the Gospel to the Apostle John, and gives an account of the circumstances under which it was written, fabulous doubtless in some of its details, but having probably a basis of truth. ||

Celsus, the celebrated heathen adversary of Christianity (A.D. 178, Keim), professedly founds his statements concerning the history of Christ on "the writings of his disciples";** and his accounts are manifestly based on our four Gospels,††

---

* *Epist.* c. 3; Routh, p. 298; Euseb. v. 1. § 10. In the same section we have other expressions apparently borrowed from John xv. 13 and 1 John iii. 16. See, further, Lightfoot's article, "The Churches of Gaul," in the *Contemp. Review* for August, 1876, xxviii. 405 ff. An English translation of the Fragments of Melito and Apollinaris, and of the Epistle of the Churches of Vienne and Lyons, will be found appended to vol. ii. of Lactantius, in vol. xxii. of the Ante-Nicene Christian Library.

† *Suppl. pro Christ.* c. 10, p. 46, ed. Otto.

‡ *Ad Autol.* ii. 22, pp. 118–120, ed. Otto.

|| See on this subject Lightfoot in the *Contemp. Review* for October, 1875, xxvi. 835 ff.; Matthew Arnold, *God and the Bible*, p. 248 (Eng. ed.); and Westcott, "Introd. to the Gospel of St. John," in *The Holy Bible . . . with . . . Commentary*, etc., ed. by F. C. Cook, *N.T.*, vol. ii. p. xxxv.; also his *Canon of the N. T.*, 5th ed., p. 214 ff.

** Origen, *Cels.* ii. 13, 74; comp. 32, 53. He quotes these writings as possessing among Christians unquestioned authority: "We need," says he, "no other witness; for you fall upon your own swords" (ii. 74).

†† See fully in Lardner, *Testimonies of Ancient Heathens*, ch. xviii., *Works*, vii. 210–278; Kirchhofer, *Quellensammlung zur Gesch. des neutest. Canons* (1844), pp. 330–349; Keim, *Celsus' Wahres Wort* (1873), pp. 223–230. Comp. Norton, *Genuineness of the Gospels*, i. 142 ff.; E. A. Abbott, art. *Gospels*, in the *Encyc. Britannica*, 9th ed., x. 818.

though he does not name their authors. He refers to several circumstances peculiar to the narrative of John, as the blood which flowed from the body of Jesus at his crucifixion,* and the fact that Christ "after his death arose, and showed the marks of his punishment, and how his hands had been pierced." † He says that "some relate that one, and some that two angels came to the sepulchre, to announce that Jesus was risen." ‡ Matthew and Mark speak of but one angel, Luke and John mention two. He says that the Jews "challenged Jesus *in the temple* to produce some clear proof that he was the Son of God." || He appears also to allude to the cry of Jesus, "I thirst," recorded only by John.** Referring to a declaration of Jesus, he satirically exclaims, "O Light and Truth!" designations of Christ characteristic of John's Gospel.†† He says that Jesus "after rising from the dead showed himself secretly to one woman only, and to his boon companions."‡‡ Here the first part of the statement seems to refer to John's account of the appearance of Christ to Mary Magdalene.

The heretical writings of this period clearly recognize the Fourth Gospel. Notwithstanding several apparent quotations or allusions, it was formerly maintained that the author of the Clementine Homilies could not possibly have used this Gospel, it being in such opposition to his opinions. But since the discovery of the Codex Ottobonianus, containing the missing portion of the book (first published by Dressel in his edition of the Homilies in 1853), there has been a change of view. That portion contains so clear a quotation of John ix. 1–3 (*Hom.* xix. 22) that Hilgenfeld has handsomely retracted his denial;|||| and, though Scholten and *Supernatu-*

*Origen, *Cels.* ii. 36, also i. 66; comp. John xix. 34.

†Origen, *Cels.* ii. 55, 59; John xx. 25, 27.

‡Origen, *Cels.* v. 52, 56; John xx. 12; comp. Luke xxiv. 4, 23.

||Origen, *Cels.* i. 67; John ii. 18; comp. x. 23, 24. (Matt. xxi. 23.)

**Origen, *Cels.* ii. 37; John xix. 28.

††Origen, *Cels.* ii. 49; John viii. 12; ix. 5; xii. 46; xiv. 6.

‡‡Origen, *Cels.* ii. 70; John xx. 14–18. Compare, however, the Addition to Mark, xvi. 9.

|||| *Einleit. in d. N.T.*, p. 43 f., note; comp. Matthew Arnold, *God and the Bible*, p. 277. Volkmar also recognizes the use of the Fourth Gospel here, but only as "an unapostolic *novum*"

ral Religion still resist the evidence, there can be little doubt about the final verdict of impartial criticism. Besides this passage and that about the new birth,* the Gospel of John seems to be used twice in *Hom.* iii. 52, once in a free quotation: "I am the gate of life; he that entereth in through me entereth into life, for there is no other teaching that can save" (comp. John x. 9, 10); and again, "My sheep hear my voice" (comp. John x. 27).

More important, and beyond any dispute, is the evidence of the use of the Fourth Gospel as the work of the Apostle John by the Gnostics of this period. Ptolemy, the disciple of Valentinus, in his Epistle to Flora, preserved by Epiphanius (*Hær.* xxxiii. 3), quotes John i. 3 as what "the Apostle says"; † and, in the exposition of the Ptolemæo-Valentinian system given by Irenæus, a long passage is quoted from Ptolemy or one of his school in which he is represented as saying that "John, the disciple of the Lord, supposes a certain Beginning," etc., citing and commenting on John i. 1–5, 14, 18, in support of the Valentinian doctrine of the Ogdoad. ‡ The Valentinians, indeed, as we are told by Irenæus elsewhere, used the Gospel of John most abundantly (*Hær.* iii. 11. § 7). Heracleon, another disciple of Valentinus, wrote a commentary on it, large extracts from which are preserved by Origen. ‖ The book commonly cited as *Excerpta Theodoti* or *Doctrina Orientalis*, a compilation (with criticisms) from the writings of Theodotus and other Gnostics of the second century, ascribed to Clement of Alexandria and

(*Ursprung uns. Evv.*, 1866, p. 62 f., 134 f.). The question is well treated by Sanday, *The Gospels in the Second Century*, pp. 293 ff. It is to be observed that the incident of "*the* man blind from his birth" is introduced in the Homilies (xix. 22) as it is in the Apostolical Constitutions (v. 7. § 17) with the use of the definite article, as something well-known to the readers of the book. How does this happen, if the writer is taking it from "an unapostolic *novum*"? Drummond and Sanday have properly called attention to this use of the article.

* *Hom.* xi. 26; see above, pp. 29, 31.

† I follow the text of Dindorf in his edition of Epiphanius, vol. ii., pp. 199, 200, who reads *τά τε πάντα* for *ἅτε πάντα* and *γεγονέναι οὐδέν* for *γέγονεν οὐδέν*.

‡ Iren. *Hær.* i. 8. § 5. The old Latin version of Irenæus, which is often more trustworthy than the Greek as preserved by Epiphanius, ends the section referred to with the words: *Et Ptolemæus quidem ita.* For the Greek, generally, see Epiphanius, *Hær.* xxxi. 27, in Dindorf's edition, which gives the best text.

‖ These are collected in Grabe's *Spicilegium SS. Patrum*, etc., ii. 85–117, 237, ed. alt. (1714), and in Stieren's Irenæus, i. 938–971.

commonly printed with his works, contains many extracts from one or more writers of the Valentinian school, in which the Gospel of John is quoted and commented upon as the work of the Apostle. (See particularly cc. 6–8, also 3, 9, 13, 17–19, 26, 41, 45, 61, 62, 65, 73.)

The literature of the third quarter of the second century is fragmentary, but we have seen that it attests the use of the Fourth Gospel in the most widely separated regions of the Christian world, and by parties diametrically opposed in sentiment. The fact that this Gospel was used by those to whose opinions it was or seemed to be adverse — by the author of the Clementine Homilies, by Quartodecimans and their opponents, and especially by the Gnostics, who were obliged to wrest its language so violently to accommodate it to their systems — shows that to have won such a reception at that time it must have come down from an earlier period with commanding authority. Its use in Tatian's Diatessaron also makes this evident. It must have belonged to those "Memoirs" to which Justin appealed fifteen or twenty years before, and which were recognized by the Christians generally of his day as the authentic sources of information respecting the life and teaching of Christ. The particular evidence we have been examining, limited as it is by the scantiness of the literature, strengthens the general conclusion before drawn from the universal reception of our four Gospels in the time of Irenæus, and from the direct indications of the use of the Fourth Gospel by Justin. The evidence that this Gospel was one of his "Memoirs" is thus cumulative, and, unless it is countervailed by some very strong objections, must be regarded as decisive. Let us then consider the main objections which have been urged against this conclusion.

The first is that, according to *Supernatural Religion*, "The description which Justin gives of the manner of the teaching of Jesus excludes the idea that he knew the Fourth Gospel. 'Brief and concise were the sentences uttered by him: for he was no Sophist, but his word was the power of God.'

No one could for a moment assert that this applies to the long and artificial discourses of the Fourth Gospel." *

Here we may observe, in the first place, that Justin's Greek is not quite accurately translated. † The word rendered "sentences" is without the article; and Prof. Drummond translates the clause more correctly, "Brief and concise sayings have proceeded from him," remarking that "Justin is describing not the universal, but only the prevailing and prominent character of his teaching." ‡ And it is not a description of the teaching in the Fourth Gospel in particular, but a general statement, not inconsistent with the fact that the character of the discourses in the Fourth Gospel is in some respects peculiar. But, as to "brief and concise sayings" of Jesus, Professor Drummond, in glancing over the first thirteen chapters of John, finds no less than fifty-three to which this description would apply. He observes that "the book contains in reality very little connected argumentation; and even the longest discourses consist rather of successive pearls of thought strung on a thread of association than of consecutive discussion and proof." ‖ But it may be greatly doubted whether Justin means here by βραχεῖς λόγοι, as Tayler supposes, simply "short, aphoristic maxims." The reference to the Sophists, that is, rhetoricians, leads one rather to suppose that Justin is contrasting the λόγοι, "discourses," of Christ in general with the long, artificial, argumentative, and rhetorical λόγοι of the Sophists among his earlier or later contemporaries, such as Dion Chrysostomus, Herodes Atticus, Polemo and Aristides, whom Philostratus describes in his biographies. As for brevity, the discourses in the Fourth Gospel are generally short: the longest continuous discourse there recorded

* *Sup. Rel.*, ii. 314; similarly J. J. Tayler, *An Attempt to ascertain the Character of the Fourth Gospel* (1867), p. 64; Davidson, *Introd. to the Study of the N.T.* (1868), ii. 386, and many others.

† *Apol.* i. 14: *βραχεῖς δὲ καὶ σύντομοι παρ' αὐτοῦ λόγοι γεγόνασιν.* It may be thought, perhaps, that *οἱ* has dropped out after *σύντομοι*, which might easily have happened. But, even if the article had been used, the argument would be worthless. Such general propositions are seldom to be taken without qualification.

‡ *Theol. Review*, July, 1877, xiv. 330.

‖ *Ibid.* pp. 330, 331.

would hardly occupy five minutes in the reading. The Sermon on the Mount as given by Matthew is much longer than any unbroken discourse in John. But what characterizes the teaching of Christ in the Gospels, as Justin intimates, is the divine authority and spiritual power with which he speaks; and this is not less striking in the Fourth Gospel than in the Synoptists. (Comp. Matt. vii. 29; Luke iv. 32; John vii. 26, 46.)

A more plausible objection is this. If Justin knew and used the Fourth Gospel at all, why has he not used it more? Why has he never appealed to it in proof of his doctrine of the Logos and of the pre-existence of Christ? He has expressly quoted but one saying of Christ recorded in it, and one of John the Baptist, and has referred to but one incident peculiar to it, unless we adopt the view of Professor Drummond respecting his reference to John xix. 13. (See above, p. 52.) His account of Christ's life and teaching corresponds substantially with that given in the Synoptic Gospels, which he follows (so it is affirmed) where they differ, or seem to differ, from John. Albrecht Thoma, in an article in Hilgenfeld's *Zeitschrift*, comes to the conclusion, after a minute examination of the subject, that Justin "knows and uses almost every chapter of the Logos-Gospel, and in part very fully." But such considerations as I have mentioned convince him, notwithstanding, that he did not regard it as apostolic, or historically authentic. He finds Justin's relation to the Apostle Paul very similar. Justin shows himself well acquainted with Paul's writings, he often follows him in his citations from the Old Testament where they differ from the Septuagint, he borrows largely his thoughts and illustrations and language, but never quotes him expressly and by name; and so Mr. Thoma thinks he cannot have regarded him as an Apostle.*

This argument forgets the nature of Justin's writings. Were he addressing a Christian community in defence of his

* See the article, "Justins literarisches Verhältniss zu Paulus und zum Johannes-Evangelium," in Hilgenfeld's *Zeitschrift für wissensch. Theologie*, 1875, xviii. 383 ff., 490 ff. The quotation in the text is from p. 553.

doctrine of the pre-existence and subordinate deity of Christ in opposition to the Ebionites, these objections would be valid. But he was writing for unbelievers. In his Apologies addressed to the Emperor and Senate and people of Rome, he cannot quote the Christian writings in *direct* proof of the truth of Christian doctrines, and makes no attempt to do so. In giving the account which he does of the teaching of Christ, he draws mainly from the Sermon on the Mount, and in his sketch of the Gospel history follows mainly the guidance of Matthew, though also using Luke, and in two or three instances Mark. That is exactly what was to be expected. Justin's chief argument is derived from the fulfilment of Old Testament prophecies, and in this he naturally follows the Gospel of Matthew, which is distinguished from the others by its reference to them. Where Matthew's citations differ from the Alexandrine version of the Old Testament, Justin often appears to borrow from Matthew rather than from the Septuagint.* The discourses of Christ as they are given in the Synoptic Gospels were obviously much better fitted for his purpose of presenting to heathens a general view of Christ's teaching than those in the Gospel of John. Similar remarks apply to the Dialogue with Trypho the Jew. Here Dr. Davidson thinks it strange that Justin should not have quoted the prologue of the Fourth Gospel, and such a passage as "Before Abraham was, I am," in proof of Christ's divinity and pre-existence.† But the Jew with whom Justin was arguing would not have accepted an assertion of John or a declaration of Christ as a proof of its truth. So in the case of Paul's writings. Paul was not so popular among the Jews that his name would recommend the arguments or illustrations which Justin borrows from him; still less could Justin quote his Epistles in proof of doctrine in a discussion with a Jew, or in a defence of Christianity addressed to heathens.

---

* See Semisch, *Die apost. Denkwürdigkeiten* u.s.w., pp. 110–120; examples are also given by Norton, *Genuineness*, etc., vol. i. Addit. Notes, pp. ccxx., ccxxii., cccxxxii. f.

† Davidson's *Introd. to the Study of the N. T.* (1868), ii. 385. Compare Volkmar, *Ueber Justin den Märtyrer* u.s.w. (Zürich, 1853), p. 20 f.; *Ursprung uns. Evang.* (1866), p. 107 f. Thoma, *ubi supra*, p. 556.

The correctness of this explanation is confirmed by an indisputable fact. Justin certainly believed that the Apostle John was the author of the Apocalypse; *Supernatural Religion* (i. 295) thinks that this was the only book of the New Testament which he regarded as "inspired"; Thoma (p. 563, note 1) even supposes that it was read in the churches in Justin's time together with the "Memoirs" and the Prophets of the Old Testament. How, then, does it happen that he has not a single quotation from this book, which calls Christ "the Word [Logos] of God" (Rev. xix. 13), "the beginning of the creation of God" (iii. 14), "the first and the last and the living one" (i. 17, comp. ii. 8), "the searcher of the reins and hearts" (ii. 23), and, apparently (though according to Alford and Westcott not really), "the Alpha and the Omega, the beginning and the end" (xxii. 13)? In speaking of the different opinions among Christians about the resurrection, Justin once refers to the book as agreeing with the prophets in predicting the Millennium, and mentions the name of the author (*Dial.* c. 81; the passage will be cited below); but, as I have said, he nowhere *quotes* this work, which he regarded as inspired, apostolic, prophetic, though it contains so much which might seem to favor his view of the person of Christ. Were it not for that almost accidental reference to it, it might be plausibly argued that he was ignorant of its existence. In one place in the Dialogue with Trypho (c. 18), Justin half apologizes for subjoining "some brief sayings" of the Saviour to the words of the Prophets, on the ground that Trypho had acknowledged that he had read the precepts of Christ "in the so-called Gospel" (*Dial.* c. 10). But he does not introduce them there as arguments.

It should be observed, further, that the course pursued by Justin in abstaining from quoting the Gospels in proof of doctrines, and in not mentioning the Evangelists by name, in writings addressed to unbelievers, is simply that which was followed, with slight exceptions, by a long line of Christian Apologists from his time down to that of Eusebius.*

* See Norton, *Gen. of the Gospels*, i. 218 ff.; Westcott, *Canon of the N.T.*, p. 116 ff.; E. S. Ffoulkes, art. *Fathers*, in Smith and Wace's *Dict. of Christian Biog.*, ii. 456 f.

It may still be said that this applies only to quotations made in proof of *doctrines*. It may be asked, and there is some force in the question, Why has not Justin used John as he has used the Synoptic Gospels, as an authority for historical facts, for facts which he supposed to be predicted in the Old Testament? To take one example which has been urged: Justin has quoted from the Old Testament, in precisely the same form as John (differing from the established text of the Septuagint), the words, "They shall look on me whom they pierced": * but instead of referring to the incident which led John to quote it,—the thrusting of a spear into our Saviour's side by a Roman soldier,—he seems to apply it to the crucifixion generally. How could he do this, if he accepted the Gospel of John? †

This case presents little difficulty. The verbs in the quotation, it will be observed, are in the plural. If Justin regarded the prophecy as including the act of the Roman soldier, he could not have restricted it to that: he must have regarded the language of the Old Testament as referring also to the piercing of the hands and the feet of Jesus on the part of the soldiers who nailed him to the cross. It is not strange, therefore, that he should quote the passage without referring to the particular act mentioned by John. He applies the prophecy, moreover, to the Jews, who *caused* the death of Jesus, and not to the Roman soldiers, who were the immediate agents in the crucifixion. ‡

But there is a stronger case than this. Justin, who speaks of Christ as "the passover" or paschal lamb, symbolizing the deliverance of Christian believers from death, "as the blood of the passover saved those who were in Egypt" (*Dial.* c. 111, comp. 40), has not noticed the fact recorded by John alone, that the legs of Christ were not broken by the Roman soldiers at the crucifixion. This the Evangelist regards as a fulfilment of the scripture, "A bone of him shall not be

* Zech. xii. 10; John xix. 37; Justin, *Apol.* i. 52. See above, p. 48.

† Thoma, pp. 542 f., 556; comp. Engelhardt, *Das Christenthum Justins des Märtyrers* (1878), p. 350.

‡ *Apol.* i. 52; *Dial.* cc. 14, 32, 64, 118; comp. *Dial.* cc. 85, 93, etc.; Acts ii. 23; x. 39.

broken"; and this quotation is commonly referred to the direction respecting the paschal lamb (Ex. xii. 46; Num. ix. 12). How, it may be asked, could Justin, with his fondness for types, have neglected such a fulfilment as this, when the Evangelist had already pointed it out? This argument is plausible, and has some weight. Let us consider it.

In the first place, I must venture to doubt whether there is any reference to the paschal lamb in John xix. 36. The Evangelist says nothing whatever to indicate such a reference, though some explanation would seem to be needed of the transformation of a precept into a prediction. The language of Ps. xxxiv. 20 (Sept. xxxiii. 21) corresponds more closely with the citation; and, considering the free way in which passages of the Old Testament are applied in the New, the fact that in the connection in which the words stand in the Psalm protection of life is referred to does not seem a very serious objection to the supposition that the Evangelist had this passage in mind. He may well have regarded the part of the Psalm which he quotes as fulfilled in the case of "Jesus Christ the righteous" in the incident which he records, and the preceding verse as fulfilled in the resurrection. And some eminent scholars take this view of his meaning; so, *e.g.*, Grotius, Wetstein, Bishop Kidder, Hammond, Whitby, Brückner, Bäumlein, Weiss;* others, as Lenfant and Le Clerc, leave the matter doubtful; and some, as Vitringa and Bengel, suppose the Evangelist to have had both passages in mind. But, waiving this question, I would say, once for all, that very little importance is to be attached to this sort of *a priori* reasoning. We may be surprised that Justin should not have been led by the Fourth Gospel to find here a fulfilment of prophecy of some sort, and to use it in his argument; but a hundred cases equally surprising might be cited of the neglect of a writer to use an argument or to recognize a fact which we should have confidently expected that he would use or recognize. To take the first that lies at hand. I have before me the work of Dr. Sanday,

* *Bibl. Theol. des N.T.*, 3e Aufl. (1880), p. 638; comp. his *Der Johanneische Lehrbegriff* (1862), p. 114, note. So R. H. Hutton, *Essays, Theol. and Literary*, 2d ed. (1880), i. 195.

The Gospels in the Second Century, a learned, elaborate, and valuable treatise in reply to *Supernatural Religion*. He adduces from all sources the evidence of the use of the Gospels by writers who flourished in the period from Clement of Rome to Clement of Alexandria and Tertullian, including those whose references to the Gospel are very slight and doubtful, or of whom mere fragments remain. Appended to the work is a chronological and analytical table of these authors. But, on looking it over, we find no mention of Theophilus, bishop of Antioch A.D. 169–181; and Dr. Sanday has nowhere presented the testimony of this writer, though we have from him an elaborate "Apology" or defence of Christianity in three books, in which he quotes several passages from the Gospel of Matthew with the introduction, "The evangelic voice teaches" so and so, or "the Gospel says," * and though, as we have seen, he quotes the Gospel of John (ch. i. 1, 3), naming the Evangelist, and describing him as one moved by the Spirit of God (see above, p. 58). He is in fact the earliest writer who does thus expressly quote the Fourth Gospel as the work of John. Now suppose Dr. Sanday was a Father of the third or fourth century who had composed a treatise with the purpose of collecting the evidences of the use of the Gospels by early Christian writers. What would the author of *Supernatural Religion* say to the facts in this case? Would he not argue that Sandæus could not possibly have been acquainted with this work of Theophilus, and that the pretended "Apology" was probably spurious? And, if he found in Sandæus (p. 303) a single apparent allusion to that writer, would he not maintain that this must be an interpolation?—Or to take another example. Sandæus is examining the question about Justin Martyr's use of the Gospels, and observes that "he says emphatically that all the children (πάντας ἁπλῶς τοὺς παῖδας) in Bethlehem were slain, without mentioning the limitation of age given in St. Matthew" (p. 106; comp. Justin, *Dial.* c. 78). Now in our present texts of Justin there is another

---

* *Ad Autol.* lib. iii. cc. 13, 14, ed. Otto; comp. Matt. v. 28, 44, 46; vi. 3.

reference to the slaughter of the innocents, in which Herod is represented as "destroying all the children born in Bethlehem *at that time*." * But here *Supernatural Religion* might argue, It is certain that this qualifying phrase could not have been in the copy used by Sandæus, who takes no notice of the passage, though his aim is to meet the objections to the genuineness of our Gospels. Is it not clear that the words were interpolated by some one who wished to bring Justin into harmony with Matthew? Would Justin be so inconsistent with himself as that addition would make him?

A multitude of questions may be asked, to which no particular answer can be given, in reference to the use which Justin and writers in all ages have made of our Gospels. We cannot say why he has quoted this saying of Jesus and not that, or referred to this incident in the history and not that; why, for example, in his account of Christ's teaching in his First Apology, he makes no allusion to any of the parables which form so remarkable a feature of it, and quotes from them in but one place in his Dialogue with Trypho (*Dial.* c. 125). We can only say that he had to stop somewhere; † that he has used the Gospels much more freely than any other of the many Christian Apologists whose writings have come down to us from his day to that of Lactantius and Eusebius; that his selection of the sayings of Christ seems on the whole judicious and natural, though many pearls of great price are missing; that the historical incidents by which he supports his special argument from the fulfilment of prophecy are for the most part what might be expected; and that it was natural that in general he should follow the Synoptic Gospels rather than that of John.‡ But one needs only to try experiments on particular works by almost any writer to find that great caution is required in drawing inferences from what he has *not* done.

---

* *Dial.* c. 103: *ἀνελόντος πάντας τοὺς ἐν Βηθλεὲμ ἐκείνου τοῦ καιροῦ γεννηθέντας παῖδας.*

† Comp. *Apol.* i. 53: "Here we conclude, though we have many other prophecies to produce."

‡ See on this point Meyer, *Komm. über d. Ev. Joh.*, 5e Aufl. (1869), p. 8 f., note (Eng. trans., p. 8 f., note 3); comp. Weizsäcker, *Untersuchungen über d. evang. Geschichte*, p. 229.

As to the case before us, Justin may not have thought of the incident peculiar to the Fourth Gospel, or he may have considered, and very reasonably too, that an argument for the typical character of the paschal lamb founded on the direction given in the Pentateuch about the bones, or an argument *assuming* the Messianic reference of the passage in the Psalms, was not well adapted to convince unbelievers. Perhaps he had urged this argument in the actual dialogue with Trypho, and had encountered objections to its validity which he did not find it easy to answer. This may seem more probable than the supposition of forgetfulness. But will you say that such a failure of memory as has been suggested is incredible? Let us compare a case. One of the most distinguished scholars of this country, in an article published in the American Biblical Repository, remarks, in the course of an elaborate argument: —

> The particulars inserted or omitted by different Evangelists vary exceedingly from each other, some inserting what others omit, and some narrating at length what others briefly touch. *E.g.*, compare the history of the temptation by Mark, and even by Matthew and Luke; and where is the history of the *transfiguration* to be found, except in Matthew? *

Could anything be *a priori* more incredible than that an eminent Biblical scholar, who when this was written had held the office of Professor of Sacred Literature in the Andover Theological Seminary for nearly thirty years, should have forgotten that both Mark and Luke have given full accounts of the transfiguration, the latter especially mentioning a number of important particulars not found in Matthew? † If Professor Stuart was occasionally guilty of oversights, — as who is not? — he certainly had a clearer head and a better memory than Justin Martyr, who in quoting and referring to the Old Testament makes not a few extraordinary mistakes. ‡

I admit that some weight should be allowed to the argu-

---

* *American Biblical Repository*, October, 1838, xii. 341.

† Compare Mark ix. 2–8 and Luke ix. 28–36 with Matt. xvii. 1–8.

‡ See the references already given, p. 49, note *; also *Some Account of the Writings and Opinions of Justin Martyr*, by John [Kaye], Bishop of Lincoln, 3d ed. (1853), pp. 139 f. 148; comp. p. 129 f.

ment we have been examining, so far as reference to the history in the Gospel of John is concerned; but it does not seem to me that much importance should be attached to it. The tradition in the Synoptic Gospels represents without doubt the substance of the apostolic preaching; it was earlier committed to writing than that contained in the Fourth Gospel; the incidents of the threefold narrative were more familiar; and the discourses, especially, as has already been remarked, were far better fitted for illustrating the general character of Christ's teaching than those of the Fourth Gospel. It would have been very strange, therefore, if in such works as those of Justin the Synoptic Gospels had not been mainly used.

Engelhardt, the most recent writer on Justin, is impressed by the facts which Thoma presents respecting Justin's relation to John, but comes to a different conclusion. He thinks Justin could never have made the use of John's Gospel which he has done, if he had not regarded it as genuine. It purports to be a work of the beloved disciple. The conjecture that by "the disciple whom Jesus loved" Andrew was intended (Lützelberger), or Nathanael (Spaeth), or a personified ideal conception (Scholten), was reserved for the sagacity of critics of the nineteenth century: there is no trace that in Christian antiquity this title ever suggested any one but John. The Gospel must have been received as his work, or rejected as fictitious. Engelhardt believes that Justin received it, and included it in his "Memoirs"; but he conjectures that with it there was commonly read in the churches and used by Justin a Harmony of the first three Gospels, or at least of Matthew and Luke, while the Fourth Gospel, not yet incorporated into the Harmony, stood in the background.* I do not feel the need of this hypothesis; but it may deserve consideration.

It is objected further that Justin's statements repeatedly contradict the Fourth Gospel, and that he cannot therefore have regarded it as apostolic or authentic. For example, he follows the Synoptic Gospels, so Hilgenfeld and David-

* See Engelhardt, *Das Christenthum Justins des Märtyrers*, pp. 345-352.

son and *Supernatural Religion* affirm, in placing, in opposition to John, the death of Christ on the 15th of Nisan, the day after the paschal lamb was killed.

The argument that Justin cannot have accepted the Gospel of John because he has followed the Synoptists in respect to the day of Christ's death hardly needs an answer. If the discrepancy referred to, whether real or not, did not prevent the whole Christian world from accepting John and the Synoptic Gospels alike in the last quarter of the second century, it need not have hindered Justin from doing so at an earlier date. But it is far from certain that Hilgenfeld and Davidson have correctly interpreted the language of Justin: "It is written that you seized him on the day of the passover, and in like manner crucified him at [*or* during] the passover (ἐν τῷ πάσχα)."* Meyer understands this as placing the death of Jesus on the day of the passover; † Otto in an elaborate note on the passage in his *third* edition of Justin's Works maintains the same view; ‡ Thoma regards the language as ambiguous.|| I will not undertake to pronounce an opinion upon so difficult a question, as the objection is futile on any supposition.

Again, *Supernatural Religion* asserts that "Justin contradicts the Fourth Gospel, in limiting the work of Jesus to one year." (*S. R.* ii. 313.) Dr. Davidson makes the same statement; ** but neither he nor *S. R.* adduces any proof of it. I know of no passage in Justin which affirms or implies this limitation. But, if such a passage should be found, the argument against Justin's reception of the Fourth Gospel would

---

* *Dial.* c. 111. See Hilgenfeld, *Der Paschastreit der alten Kirche* (1860), pp. 205-209; Davidson, *Introd. to the Study of the N.T.* (1868), ii. 384; *Sup. Rel.*, ii. 313; comp. Wieseler, *Beiträge* (1869), p. 240.—Note here the use of γέγραπται.

† *Komment. üb. d. Ev. des Joh.*, 5e Aufl. p. 24 f. (Eng. trans. i. 24 f.) Steitz, who formerly agreed with Hilgenfeld, afterwards adopted the view of Meyer; see the art. *Pascha* in Herzog's *Real-Encyk. f. Prot. u. Kirche*, xi. 151, note *.

‡ *Iustini . . . Martyris Opera*, tom. i. pars ii, ed. tert. (1877), p. 395 f. Otto cites *Dial.* c. 99, where the agony in Gethsemane is referred to as taking place "on the day on which Jesus was to be crucified," as showing that Justin followed the Jewish reckoning of the day from sunset to sunset. Davidson takes no notice of this. If Meyer and Otto are right, we have here a strong argument for Justin's use of the Fourth Gospel.

|| *Ubi supra*, p. 535 f.

** *Introd. to the Study of the N.T.*, ii. 387.

be worthless. The opinion that Christ's ministry lasted but one year, or little more, was held by many in the early Church who received the Gospel of John without question. It was maintained by the Basilidians, the Valentinians, and the author of the Clementine Homilies, by Clement of Alexandria, Tertullian, Origen, Julius Africanus, Pseudo-Cyprian, Archelaus, Lactantius, Ephraem Syrus apparently, Philastrius, Gaudentius, Q. Julius Hilarianus, Augustine apparently, Evagrius the presbyter, and others among the Fathers, and has been held by modern scholars, as Bentley, Mann, Priestley (*Harmony*), Lant Carpenter (*Harmony*), and Henry Browne (*Ordo Sæclorum*).* The Fathers were much influenced by their interpretation of Isa. lxi. 2, — "to preach the acceptable year of the Lord," — quoted in Luke iv. 19. It is true that John vi. 4 is against this view; but its defenders find means, satisfactory to themselves, of getting over the difficulty.

Other objections urged by Dr. Davidson and *Supernatural Religion* seem to me too weak to need an answer. I will, however, notice one which is brought forward with great confidence by Thoma, who says "Justin directly contradicts the Fourth Gospel" (p. 556), and after him by F. C. J. van Goens, who introduces it with the words *enfin et surtout*.†

---

* The Basilidians, see Clem. Alex. *Strom.* i. 21, p. 408.—Valentinians, see Iren. *Hær.* i. 3. (al. 5), § 3; ii. 20. (al. 36), § 1; 22. (al. 38–40), §§ 1–6.—Clem. Hom. xvii. 19.—Clem. Alex. *Strom.* i. 21, p. 407; vi. 11, p. 783, l. 40; comp. v. 6, p. 668; vii. 17, p. 898.—Tertull. *Adv. Jud.* c. 8; *Marc.* i. 15 (but here are different readings).—Origen, *De Princip.* iv. 5, Opp. i. 160; *In Levit. Hom.* ix. c. 5, Opp. ii. 239; *In Luc. Hom.* xxxii., Opp. iii. 970; contra, *In Matt. Comm. Ser.*, c. 40, Opp. iii. 859, "fere tres annos"; comp. *Cels.* ii. 12, Opp. i. 397, οὐδὲ τρία ἔτη.—Jul. Africani *Chron.* frag. l. ap. Routh, *Rell. Sacræ*, ii. 301 f., ed. alt.—Pseudo-Cyprian, *De Paschæ Comp.* (A.D. 243), c. 22.—Archelai et Manetis Disp., c. 34.—Lactant. *Inst.* iv. 10. (*De Morte Persec.* c. 2.)—Ephraem, *Serm.* xiii. *in Nat. Dom.*, Opp. Syr. ii. 432.—Philastr. *Hær.* 106.—Gaudent. *Serm.* iii., Migne, *Patrol. Lat.* xx. 865.—Hilarianus, *De Mundi Dur.* (A.D. 397) c. 16; *De Die Paschæ*, c. 15; Migne, xiii. 1104, 1114, or Gallandi, *Bibl. Patr.* viii. 238, 748.—Augustine, *De Civ. Dei*, xviii. 54, Opp. vii. 866; *Ad Hesych. Epist.* 199 (al. 80), § 20, Opp. ii. 1122; contra, *De Doct. Christ.* ii. 42 (al. 28), Opp. iii. 66.—Evagrius presbyter (*cir.* A.D. 423), *Alterc. inter Theoph. Christ. et Sim. Jud.*, Migne xx. 1176, or Gallandi, ix. 254.—So also the author of the treatise *De Promissis et Prædictionibus Dei* (published with the works of Prosper Aquitanus), pars i. c. 7; pars v. c. 2; Migne, li. 739 c, 855 b.—Browne, *Ordo Sæclorum* (Corrections and Additions), also cites Cyril of Alexandria, *In Isa.* xxxii. 10, Opp. ii. 446 d e, but this rests on a false inference; see, *contra*, Cyril, *In Isa.* xxix. 1, Opp. ii. 408 b. Besides the works of Nicholas Mann, *De veris Annis Jesu Christi natali et emortuali*, Lond. 1752, p. 158 ff., Greswell, *Dissertations*, etc., i. 438 ff., 2d ed. (1837), and Henry Browne, *Ordo Sæclorum*, Lond. 1844, p. 80 ff., one may consult especially F. X. Patritius (*i.e.* Patrizi), *De Evangeliis* (Friburg. Brisgov. 1853), lib. iii., diss. xix., p. 171 ff.

† *Revue de théologie et de philosophie*, Lausanne, 1878, xi. 92 f.

Justin speaks of Christ as "keeping silence and refusing any longer to make any answer to any one before Pilate, as has been declared in the Memoirs by the Apostles" (*Dial.* c. 102). M. van Goens remarks, "No one who had ever read the Fourth Gospel could speak in this way." What does M. van Goens think of Tertullian, who says,* "Velut agnus coram tondente se sine voce, sic non aperuit os suum. Hic enim *Pilato interrogante nihil locutus est*"? If Justin had even said that Christ made no answer when Pilate questioned him, this would be sufficiently explained by John xix. 9, to which Tertullian perhaps refers. But the expressions "no longer" and "*before* Pilate" lead rather to the supposition that Justin refers to Matt. xxvii. 11–14 and Mark xv. 2–5 (οὐκέτι οὐδὲν ἀπεκρίθη, "he no longer made any answer"), which certainly there is nothing in John to contradict.

Finally, the author of *Supernatural Religion* urges, generally, that in citing the Old Testament Justin, according to Semisch's count, refers to the author by name or by book one hundred and ninety-seven times, and omits to do this only one hundred and seventeen times. On the other hand, in referring to the words of Christ or the facts of Christian history for which he relied on the "Memoirs," he never cites the book (*S. R.* regards the "Memoirs" as one book) by the name of the author, except in a single instance, where he refers to "Peter's Memoirs" (*Dial.* c. 106).† "The inference," he says, "must not only be that he attached small importance to the Memoirs, but was actually ignorant of the author's name" (*S. R.* i. 297). That Justin attached small importance to the "Memoirs by the Apostles" on which he professedly relied for the teaching and life of Christ, and this, as *S. R.* contends, to the exclusion of oral tradition (*S. R.* i. 298), is an "inference" and a proposition which would surprise us in almost any other writer. The inference, moreover, that Justin "was actually ignorant of the author's name," when in one instance, according to *S. R.*,

* *Adv. Jud.* c. 13, Opp. ii. 737, ed. Oehler.

† See above, p. 22 f.

"he indicates Peter" as the author (*S. R.* i. 285), and when, as *S. R.* maintains, "the Gospel according to Peter," or "the Gospel according to the Hebrews" (which he represents as substantially the same work), was in all probability the source from which the numerous quotations in his works differing from our Gospels are taken,* is another specimen of singular logic. So much for generalities. But a particular objection to the conclusion that the Gospel of John was one of Justin's "Memoirs" is founded on the fact that he has never quoted or referred to it under the name of the author, though he has named the Apostle John as the author of the Apocalypse. (*S. R.* i. 298.) Great stress is laid on this contrast by many writers.

Let us see to what these objections amount. In the first place, the *way* in which Justin has mentioned John as the author of the Apocalypse is in itself enough to explain why he should not have named him in citing the "Memoirs." In his Dialogue with Trypho, after having quoted prophecies of the Old Testament in proof of his doctrine of the Millennium,—a doctrine in which he confesses some Christians did not agree with him,—he wishes to state that his belief is supported by a Christian writing which he regards as inspired and prophetic. He accordingly refers to the work as follows: "And afterwards also a certain man among us, whose name was John, one of the Apostles of Christ, in a revelation made by him prophesied that the believers in our Christ should spend a thousand years in Jerusalem," etc. (*Dial.* c. 81.) The Apostle John was certainly as well known outside of the Christian body as any other of the Evangelists; but we see that he is here introduced to Trypho as a stranger. Still more would he and the other Evangelists be strangers to the Roman Emperor and Senate, to whom the Apologies were addressed. That Justin under such circumstances should quote the Evangelists by name, assigning this saying or incident to "the Gospel according to Matthew," that to "Luke," and the other to "the Gospel according to John,"

* *Supernatural Religion*, i. 321; comp. pp. 312, 323, 332, 398, 416, 418–427; ii. 311, 7th ed.

as if he were addressing a Christian community familiar with the books, would have been preposterous. Justin has *described* the books in his First Apology as Memoirs of Christ, resting on the authority of the Apostles, and received by the Christians of his time as authentic records. That was all that his purpose required: the names of four unknown persons would have added no weight to his citations. In the Dialogue, he is even more specific in his description of the "Memoirs" than in the Apology. But to suppose that he would quote them as he quotes the books of the Old Testament with which Trypho was familiar is to ignore all the proprieties and congruities of the case.

This view is confirmed and the whole argument of *Supernatural Religion* is nullified by the fact that the general practice of Christian Apologists down to the time of Eusebius corresponds with that of Justin, as we have before had occasion to remark. (See above, p. 67.) It may be added that, while in writings addressed to Christian readers by the earlier Fathers the Old Testament is often, or usually, cited with reference to the author or book, the cases are comparatively very rare in which the Evangelists are named. For example, Clement of Alexandria, according to Semisch, quotes the Old Testament writers or books far oftener than otherwise by name, while in his very numerous citations from the Gospels he names John but three times, Matthew twice, Luke twice, and Mark once; in the countless citations of the Gospels in the Apostolical Constitutions, the Evangelists are never named; and so in the numerous quotations of the Gospels in Cyprian's writings, with the exception of a single treatise (the *Testimonia* or *Ad Quirinum*), the names of the Evangelists are never mentioned. But it cannot be necessary to expose further the utter futility of this objection, which has so often been inconsiderately urged.*

In this view of the objections to the supposition that Justin used the Gospel of John and included it in his

* See Semisch, *Die apostol. Denkwürdigkeiten*, u. s. w., p. 84 ff.; and compare Norton, *Genuineness*, etc., i. 205 ff., 2d ed.

"Memoirs," I have either cited them in the precise language of their authors, or have endeavored to state them in their most plausible form. When fairly examined, only one of them appears to have weight, and that not much. I refer to the objection that, if Justin used the Fourth Gospel at all, we should expect him to have used it more. It seems to me, therefore, that there is nothing of importance to countervail the very strong presumption from different lines of evidence that the "Memoirs" of Justin Martyr, "composed by Apostles and their companions," were our four Gospels.

A word should perhaps be added in reference to the view of Dr. E. A. Abbott, in the valuable article *Gospels* contributed to the new edition of the Encyclopædia Britannica. He holds that Justin's "Memoirs" included the first three Gospels, and these only. These alone were received by the Christian community of his time as the authentic records of the life and teaching of Christ. If so, how can we explain the fact that a pretended Gospel so different in character from these, and so inconsistent with them as it is supposed to be, should have found universal acceptance in the next generation on the part of Christians of the most opposite opinions, without trace of controversy, with the slight exception of the Alogi previously mentioned? *

I have not attempted in the present paper a thorough discussion of Justin Martyr's quotations, but only to illustrate by some decisive examples the false assumptions on which the reasoning of *Supernatural Religion* is founded. In a full treatment of the subject, it would be necessary to consider the question of Justin's use of apocryphal Gospels, and in particular the "Gospel according to the Hebrews" and the "Gospel according to Peter," which figure so prominently in what calls itself "criticism" (*die Kritik*) as the pretended source of Justin's quotations. This subject has already been

* See above, p. 20. The work of Hippolytus, of which we know only the title found on the cathedra of his statue at Rome, "On [*or* "In defence of" (ὑπὲρ)] the Gospel according to John and the Apocalypse," may have been written in answer to their objections. See Bunsen's *Hippolytus*, 2d ed. (1854), i. 460. On the Alogi see also Weizsäcker, *Untersuchungen über d. evang. Geschichte*, p. 226 f., note.

referred to;* but it is impossible to treat it here in detail. In respect to "the Gospel according to the Hebrews" I will give in a Note some quotations from the article *Gospels, Apocryphal*, by Professor R. A. Lipsius, of Jena, in the second volume of Smith and Wace's *Dictionary of Christian Biography*, published in the present year, with extracts from other recent writers, which will sufficiently show how groundless is the supposition that Justin's quotations were mainly derived from this Gospel.† Lipsius certainly will not be suspected of any "apologetic" tendency. Credner's hypothesis that the "Gospel according to Peter," which he regards as the Gospel used by the Jewish Christians generally, and strangely identifies with the *Diatessaron* of Tatian, was the chief source of Justin's quotations, was thoroughly refuted by Mr. Norton as long ago as the year 1834 in the *Select Journal of Foreign Periodical Literature*, and afterwards in a Note to the first edition of his work on the Genuineness of the Gospels.‡ It is exposed on every side to overwhelming objections, and has hardly a shadow of evidence to support it. Almost our whole knowledge of this Gospel is derived from the account of it by Serapion, bishop of Antioch near the end of the second century (A.D. 191–213), who is the first writer by whom it is mentioned.|| He "found it for the most part in accordance with the right doctrine of the Saviour," but containing passages favoring the opinions of the Docetæ, by whom it was used. According to Origen, it represented the "brethren" of Jesus as sons of Joseph by a former wife.** It was evidently a book of very little note. Though it plays a conspicuous part in the speculations of modern German scholars and of *Supernatural Religion* about

---

* See above, p. 17 f.

† See Note C, at the end of this essay.

‡ *Select Journal*, etc. (Boston), April, 1834, vol iii., part ii., pp. 234–242; *Evidences of the Genuineness of the Gospels*, vol. i. (1837), Addit. Notes, pp. ccxxxii.-cclv. See also Bindemann, who discusses ably the whole question about Justin Martyr's Gospels, in the *Theol. Studien u. Kritiken*, 1842, pp. 355–482; Semisch, *Die apostol. Denkwürdigkeiten* u. s. w, pp. 43–59; on the other side, Credner, *Beiträge* u. s. w., vol. i (1832); Mayerhoff, *Hist.-crit. Einleitung in die petrinischen Schriften* (1835), p. 234 ff.; Hilgenfeld, *Krit. Untersuchungen* u. s. w., p. 259 ff.

|| Serapion's account of it is preserved by Eusebius, *Hist. Eccl.* vi. 12.

** Origen, *Comm. in Matt.* t. x. § 17, Opp. iii. 462 f.

the origin of the Gospels and the quotations of Justin Martyr, *not a single fragment of it has come down to us.* This *nominis umbra* has therefore proved wonderfully convenient for those who have had occasion, in support of their hypotheses, "to draw unlimited cheques," as Lightfoot somewhere expresses it, "on the bank of the unknown." Mr. Norton has shown, by an acute analysis of Serapion's account of it, that in all probability it was not an historical, but a doctrinal work.* Lipsius remarks: "The statement of Theodoret (*Hær. Fab.* ii. 2) that the Nazarenes had made use of this Gospel rested probably on a misunderstanding. The passage moreover in Justin Martyr (*Dial. c. Tryph.* 106) in which some have thought to find mention of the *Memorials of Peter* is very doubtful. . . . Herewith fall to the ground all those hypotheses which make the *Gospel of Peter* into an original work made use of by Justin Martyr, nigh related to the *Gospel of the Hebrews,* and either the Jewish Christian basis of our canonical St. Mark [so Hilgenfeld], or, at any rate, the Gospel of the Gnosticizing Ebionites" [Volkmar]. † To this I would only add that almost the only fact of which we are directly informed respecting the contents of the so-called "Gospel of Peter" is that it favored the opinions of the Docetæ, to which Justin Martyr, who wrote a book against the Marcionites (Euseb. *Hist. Eccl.* iv. 11. § 8), was diametrically opposed.

Glancing back now over the ground we have traversed, we find (1) that the general reception of our four Gospels as sacred books throughout the Christian world in the time of Irenæus makes it almost certain that the "Memoirs called Gospels," "composed by Apostles and their companions," which were used by his early contemporary Justin Martyr, and were read in the Christian churches of his day as the authoritative records of Christ's life and teaching, were the same books; (2) that this presumption is confirmed by the actual use which Justin has made of all our Gospels, though

* *Genuineness of the Gospels,* 2d ed., vol. iii. (1848), pp. 255-260; abridged edition (1867), pp. 362-366.

† Smith and Wace's *Dict. of Christian Biog.*, ii. 712.

he has mainly followed, as was natural, the Gospel of Matthew, and his *direct* citations from the Gospel of John, and references to it, are few; (3) that it is still further strengthened, in respect to the Gospel of John, by the evidences of its use between the time of Justin and that of Irenæus, both by the Catholic Christians and the Gnostics, and especially by its inclusion in Tatian's *Diatessaron;* (4) that, of the two principal assumptions on which the counter-argument is founded, one is demonstrably false and the other baseless; and (5) that the particular objections to the view that Justin included the Gospel of John in his "Memoirs" are of very little weight. We are authorized then, I believe, to regard it as in the highest degree probable, if not morally certain, that in the time of Justin Martyr the Fourth Gospel was generally received as the work of the Apostle John.

III. WE pass now to our third point, the use of the Fourth Gospel by the various Gnostic sects. The length to which the preceding discussion has extended makes it necessary to treat this part of the subject in a very summary manner.

The Gnostic sects with which we are concerned became conspicuous in the second quarter of the second century, under the reigns of Hadrian (A.D. 117–138) and Antoninus Pius (A.D. 138–161). The most prominent among them were those founded by Marcion, Valentinus, and Basilides. To these may be added the Ophites or Naassenes.

Marcion has already been referred to.* He prepared a Gospel for his followers by striking from the Gospel of Luke what was inconsistent with his system, and treated in a similar manner ten of the Epistles of Paul. He rejected the other Gospels, not on the ground that they were spurious, but because he believed their authors were under the influence of Jewish prejudices.† In proof of this, he appealed to the passage in the Epistle to the Galatians on which Baur

* See above, p. 21.

† See Irenæus, *Hær.* iii. 12. § 12.

and his school lay so much stress. "Marcion," says Tertullian, "having got the Epistle of Paul to the Galatians, who reproves even the Apostles themselves for not walking straight, according to the truth of the Gospel, . . . endeavors to destroy the reputation of those Gospels which are truly such, and are published under the name of Apostles, or also of apostolic men, in order that he may give to his own the credit which he takes away from them." * In another place, Tertullian says, addressing Marcion: "If you had not rejected some and corrupted others of the Scriptures which contradict your opinion, the Gospel of John would have confuted you." † Again: "Of those historians whom we possess, it appears that Marcion *selected* Luke for his mutilations." ‡ The fact that Marcion placed his rejection of the Gospels on this ground, that the Apostles were but imperfectly enlightened, shows that he could not question their apostolic authorship.‖ His reference to the Epistle to the Galatians indicates also that the "pillar-apostles" (Gal. ii. 9), Peter and John, were particularly in his mind. Peter, it will be remembered, was regarded as having sanctioned the Gospel of Mark. (See above, p. 23.)

It has been asserted by many modern critics, as Hilgenfeld, Volkmar, Scholten, Davidson, and others, that, if Marcion had been acquainted with the Gospel of John, he would have chosen that, rather than Luke, for expurgation, on account of its marked anti-Judaic character. But a careful comparison of John's Gospel with Marcion's doctrines will show that it contradicts them in so many places and so

---

* *Adv. Marc.* iv. 3. Comp. *Præscr.* cc. 22–24. See also Norton, *Genuineness of the Gospels*, 2d ed., iii. 206 ff., 303 ff.; or abridged edition, pp. 332 ff., 392 ff.

† *De Carne Christi*, c. 3.

‡ *Adv. Marc.* iv. 2. "Lucam videtur Marcion elegisse quem cæderet." On account of the use of *videtur* here, Dr. Davidson, following some German critics, says, "Even in speaking about Marcion's treatment of Luke, Tertullian puts it forth as a conjecture." (*Introd. to the Study of the N. T.*, ii. 305.) A *conjecture*, when Tertullian has devoted a whole book to the refutation of Marcion from those passages of Luke which he retained! The context and all the facts of the case show that no doubt can possibly have been intended; and Tertullian often uses *videri*, not in the sense of "to seem," but of "to be seen," "to be apparent." See *Apol.* c. 19; *De Orat.* c. 21; *Adv. Prax.* cc. 26, 29; *Adv. Jud.* c. 5, from Isa. i. 12; and *De Præscr.* c. 38, which has likewise been misinterpreted.

‖ Apelles, the disciple of Marcion, appears to have used the Fourth Gospel as an authority for facts; see Hippol. *Ref. Hær.* vii. 38, p. 260, l. 20; comp. John xx. 25, 27. Hippolytus says: *τῶν δὲ εὐαγγελίων ἢ τοῦ ἀποστόλου τὰ ἀρέσκοντα αὐτῷ αἱρεῖται.* Comp. Origen, *Ep. ad charos suos* in Rufinus, *Liber de adulteratione librorum Origenis*, appended to Origen, Opp. iv. 52d, ed. Delarue.

absolutely that it would have been utterly unsuitable for his purpose.*

The theosophic or speculative Gnostics, as the Ophites, Valentinians, and Basilidians, found more in John which, by ingenious interpretation, they could use in support of their systems.†

It is moreover to be observed, in regard to the Marcionites, as Mr. Norton remarks, "that their having recourse to the mutilation of Luke's Gospel shows that no other history of Christ's ministry existed more favorable to their doctrines; that, in the first half of the second century, when Marcion lived, there was no Gnostic Gospel in being to which he could appeal." ‡

We come now to Valentinus. It has already appeared that the later Valentinians, represented by Ptolemy, Heracleon, and the *Excerpta Theodoti*, received the Gospel of John without question. || The presumption is therefore obviously very strong that it was so received by the founder of the sect. ** That this was so is the representation of Tertullian. He contrasts the course pursued by Marcion and Valentinus. "One man," he says, "perverts the Scriptures with his hand, another by his exposition of their meaning. For, if it appears that Valentinus uses the entire document,—*si Valentinus integro instrumento uti videtur*,—he has yet done violence to the truth more artfully than Marcion." For Marcion, he goes on to say, openly used the knife, not the pen; Valentinus has spared the Scriptures, but explains them away, or thrusts false meanings into them.††

---

* See on this point Bleek, *Einl. in d. N. T.*, 3d ed. (1875), p. 158, ff., with Mangold's note, who remarks that "it was simply impossible for Marcion to choose the fourth Gospel" for this purpose; also Weizsäcker, *Untersuchungen über d. evang. Geschichte* (1864), p. 230, ff.; Luthardt, *Die johan. Ursprung des vierten Ev.* (1874), p. 92, or Eng. trans., p. 108 f.; Godet, *Comm. sur l'évangile de St. Jean*, 2d ed., tom. i. (1876), p. 270 f., or Eng. trans., i. 222 f.

† On the use of the N.T. by the Valentinians, see particularly G. Heinrici, *Die valentinianische Gnosis und die Heilige Schrift*, Berlin, 1871.

‡ *Genuineness of the Gospels*, 2d ed., iii. 304; abridged ed., p. 392 f.

|| See above, p. 62 f.

** On this point, see Norton, *Genuineness*, etc., 2d ed., iii. 321 f.; abridged ed., p. 403 f.

†† Tertullian, *Præscr.* c. 38. On the use of the word *videtur*, see above, p. 83, note ‡. The context shows that no doubt is intended. If, however, the word should be taken in the sense

The testimony of Tertullian is apparently confirmed by Hippolytus, who, in a professed account of the doctrines of Valentinus (*Ref. Hær.* vi. 21–37, or 16–32, Eng. trans.; comp. the introduction, § 3), says: "All the prophets, therefore, and the Law spoke from the Demiurgus, a foolish God, he says, [and spoke] as fools, knowing nothing. Therefore, says he, the Saviour says, 'All who have come before me are thieves and robbers' (John x. 8); and the Apostle, 'The mystery which was not made known to former generations'" (Eph. iii. 4, 5). Here, however, it is urged that Hippolytus, in his account of Valentinus, mixes up references to Valentinus and his followers in such a manner that we cannot be sure that, in the use of the φησί, "he says," he is not quoting from some one of his school, and not the master. A full exhibition of the facts and discussion of the question cannot be given here. I believe there is a strong presumption that Hippolytus *is* quoting from a work of Valentinus:* the regular exposition of the opinions of his disciples, Secundus, Ptolemy, and Heracleon, does not begin till afterwards, in c. 38, or c. 33 of the English translation; but it is true that, in the present text, φησί is used vaguely toward the end of c. 35, where the opinions of the Italian and Oriental schools are distinguished in reference to a certain point. I therefore do not press this quotation as *direct* proof of the use of the Fourth Gospel by Valentinus himself.

Next to Marcion and Valentinus, the most eminent among the founders of early Gnostic sects was Basilides, of Alexandria. He flourished about A.D. 125. In the Homilies on Luke generally ascribed to Origen, though some have questioned their genuineness, we are told, in an account of apocryphal Gospels, that "Basilides had the audacity to write a Gospel according to Basilides."† Ambrose and Jerome copy this account in the prefaces to their re-

of "seems," the contrast must be between the ostensible use of the Scriptures by Valentinus and his virtual rejection of them by imposing upon them a sense contrary to their teaching. Comp. Irenæus, *Hær.* iii. 12. § 12: "scripturas quidem confitentes, interpretationes vero convertunt." So *Hær.* i. 3. § 6; iii. 14. § 4.

* See esp. Lightfoot, *Colossians*, p. 266, note 1; p. 269, note 1.

† So the Greek: Origen, *Hom.* i. in *Luc.*, Opp. iii. 932, note; the Latin in Jerome's translation reads, "Ausus fuit et Basilides scribere evangelium, et suo illud nomine titulare."

spective commentaries on Luke and Matthew; but there is no other notice of such a Gospel, or evidence of its existence, in all Christian antiquity, so far as is known. The work referred to could not have been a history of Christ's ministry, set up by Basilides and his followers in opposition to the Gospels received by the catholic Christians. In that case, we should certainly have heard of it from those who wrote in opposition to his heresy; but he and his followers are, on the contrary, represented as appealing to our Gospels of Matthew, Luke, and John;* and Hippolytus states expressly that the Basilidian account of all things concerning the Saviour subsequent to the birth of Jesus agreed with that given "in the Gospels." † The origin of the error is easily explained: a work in which Basilides set forth his view of the Gospel, *i.e.* of the teaching of Christ, might naturally be spoken of as "the Gospel according to Basilides." ‡ We have an account of such a work. Agrippa Castor, a contemporary of Basilides, and who, according to Eusebius, wrote a very able refutation of him, tells us that Basilides "composed twenty-four books on the Gospel," εἰς τὸ εὐαγγέλιον.|| Clement of Alexandria, who is one of our principal authorities for his opinions, cites his Ἐξηγητικά, "Expositions," or "Interpretations," quoting a long passage from "the twenty-third book." ** In the "Dispute between Archelaus and Manes," the "thirteenth treatise" of Basilides is cited, containing an explanation of the parable of the Rich Man and Lazarus.†† I agree with Dr. Hort in thinking it exceedingly probable that the work of Basilides which Hippolytus cites so often in his account of his opinions is the same which is quoted by Clement and Archelaus, and mentioned by Agrippa Castor.‡‡ Lipsius remarks:—

* Besides the work of Hippolytus, to be further noticed, see the passages from Clement of Alexandria and Epiphanius in Kirchhofer's *Quellensammlung*, p. 415 f.

† *Ref. Hær.* c. 27, or c. 16, Eng. trans.

‡ On this use of the term "Gospel," see Norton, *Genuineness*, etc., iii. 224 ff., or abridged edition, p. 343 f.

|| Euseb. *Hist. Eccl.* iv. 7. §§ 6, 7.

** *Strom.* iv. 12, p. 599 f.

†† *Archelai et Manetis Disputatio*, c. 55, in Routh, *Rell. sacræ*, ed. alt., v. 197.

‡‡ See the art. *Basilides* in Smith and Wace's *Dict. of Christian Biog.*, vol. i. (1877), p. 271.

In any case, the work must have been an exposition of some Gospel by whose authority Basilides endeavored to establish his Gnostic doctrine. And it is anyhow most unlikely that he would have written a commentary on a Gospel of his own composition. Of our canonical Gospels, those of Matthew, Luke, and John, were used in his school; and from the fragments just referred to we may reasonably conclude that it was the Gospel of Luke on which he wrote his commentary.*

On this it may be observed, that the phrase of Agrippa Castor, "twenty-four books on *the* Gospel," excludes the idea that any particular Gospel, like that of Luke, could be intended. Such a Gospel would have been named or otherwise defined. The expression *τὸ εὐαγγέλιον*, if it refers to any book, must signify, in accordance with that use of the term which has before been illustrated,† "the Gospels" collectively. It is so understood by Norton,‡ Tischendorf, Luthardt, Godet, and others. It would not in itself *necessarily* denote precisely our *four* Gospels, though their use by Justin Martyr, and the fact that Luke and John are commented on by Basilides, and Matthew apparently referred to by him, would make it probable that they were meant.

There is, however, another sense of the word "Gospel" as used by Basilides,—namely, "the knowledge (*gnosis*) of supermundane things" (Hippol. *Ref. Hær.* vii. 27); and "the Gospel" in this sense plays a prominent part in his system as set forth by Hippolytus. The "twenty-four books on the Gospel" mentioned by Agrippa Castor, the "Expositions" or "Interpretations" of Clement, may perhaps have related to "the Gospel" in this sense. We cannot therefore, I think, argue confidently from this title that Basilides wrote a Commentary on our Four Gospels, though it naturally suggests this. It is evident, at any rate, that he supported his *gnosis* by far-fetched interpretations of the sayings of Christ as recorded in our Gospels; and that the supposition that he had a Gospel of his own composition, in the sense of a history of Christ's life and teaching, has not only no positive support of any strength, but is on various

---

* See the art. *Gospels* in the work just cited, ii. 715. Comp. Hilgenfeld, *Einl.* p. 47.

† See above, p. 24.

‡ See Norton's *Genuineness of the Gospels*, 2d ed., iii. 235–239, or abridged edition, p. 351 ff.

accounts utterly improbable. That he used an apocryphal Gospel *not* of his own composition is a supposition for which there is not a particle of evidence of any kind whatever.

I have spoken of Basilides as quoting the Gospel of John in the citations from him by Hippolytus. The passages are the following: "And this, he says, is what is said in the Gospels: 'The true light, which enlighteneth every man, was coming into the world.'" (*Ref. Hær.* vii. 22, or c. 10, Eng. trans.) The words quoted agree exactly with John i. 9 in the Greek, though I have adopted a different construction from that of the common version in translating. Again, "And that each thing, he says, has its own seasons, the Saviour is a sufficient witness, when he says, 'My hour is not yet come.'" (*Ref. Hær.* vii. 27, al. 15; John ii. 4.)

Here two objections are raised: first, that we cannot infer from the φησί, "he says," that Hippolytus is quoting from a treatise by Basilides himself; and, secondly, that the system of Basilides as set forth by Hippolytus represents a later development of the original scheme,—in other words, that he is quoting the writings and describing the opinions of the disciples of the school, and not of its founder.

To analyze the account of Hippolytus and give the reasons for taking a different view would require an article by itself, and cannot be undertaken here. But on the first point I will quote a writer who will not be suspected of an "apologetic" tendency, Matthew Arnold. He says:—

It is true that the author of the *Philosophumena* [another name for the "Refutation of all Heresies" commonly ascribed to Hippolytus] sometimes mixes up the opinions of the master of a school with those of his followers, so that it is difficult to distinguish between them. But, if we take all doubtful cases of the kind and compare them with our present case, we shall find that it is not one of them. It is not true that here, where the name of Basileides has come just before, and where no mention of his son or of his disciples has intervened since, there is any such ambiguity as is found in other cases. It is not true that the author of the *Philosophumena* wields the *subjectless he says* in the random manner alleged, with no other formula for quotation both from the master and from the followers. In general, he uses the formula *according to them* (κατ' αὐτούς) when he quotes from the school, and the formula *he says* (φησί) when he gives the dicta of the master. And in this particular case he manifestly quotes the dicta of Basileides, and no one who had not a theory to serve would ever dream of doubting it. Basileides, therefore, about the year 125 of our era, had before him the Fourth Gospel.*

On the second point, the view that Hippolytus as contrasted with Irenæus has given an account of the system of Basilides himself is the prevailing one among scholars: it is held, for example, by Jacobi, Bunsen, Baur, Hase, Uhlhorn, Möller, Mansel, Pressensé, and Dr. Hort. The principal representative of the opposite opinion is Hilgenfeld, with whom agree Lipsius, Volkmar, and Scholten.† Dr. Hort has discussed the matter very ably and fairly in his article *Basilides* in Smith and Wace's *Dictionary of Christian Biography;* and, so far as I can judge, his conclusions are sound.

In view of all the evidence, then, I think we have good reason for believing that the Gospel of John was one of a collection of Gospels, probably embracing our four, which Basilides and his followers received as authoritative about the year 125.

The first heretics described by Hippolytus are the Oriental Gnostics,—the Ophites, or Naassenes, and the Peratæ, a kindred sect. They are generally regarded as the earliest Gnostics. Hippolytus cites from their writings numerous quotations from the Gospel of John.‡ But it is the view of many scholars that Hippolytus is really describing the opinions and quoting the writings of the later representatives of these sects.|| Not having investigated this point sufficiently, I shall argue only from what is undisputed.

Were I undertaking a full discussion of the external evidences of John's authorship of the Fourth Gospel, it would be necessary to consider here some questions about Papias,

* Matthew Arnold, *God and the Bible* (1875), p. 268 f., Eng. ed. See, to the same effect, Weizsäcker, *Untersuchungen* u. s. w., p. 232 ff. Compare Dr. Hort, art. *Basilides* in Smith and Wace's *Dict. of Christian Biog.*, i. 271, and Westcott, *Canon of the N. T.*, 4th ed., p. 288. On the other side, see Scholten, *Die ältesten Zeugnisse* u. s. w. (1867), p. 65 f.; *Sup. Rel.*, ii. 51, 7th ed., and the writers there cited.

† The two most recent discussions are that by Jacobi, in Brieger's *Zeitschrift für Kirchengeschichte*, 1876–77, i. 481–544, and, on the other side, by Hilgenfeld, in his *Zeitschrift f. wiss. Theol.*, 1878, xxi. 228–250, where the literature of the subject is given pretty fully. Moeller, in a brief notice of the two articles (Brieger's *Zeitschrift*, 1877–78, ii. 422), adheres to his former view, *versus* Hilgenfeld.

‡ *Ref. Hær.* v. 7–9 (Naassenes), 12, 16, 17 (Peratæ).

|| See Lipsius in Hilgenfeld's *Zeitschr.*, 1863, p. 410 f; 1864, p. 37 f.

and his use of the First Epistle of John, as reported by Eusebius; also the apparent reference to the First Epistle of John by Polycarp, and his relation to Irenæus; and, further, to notice the Ignatian Epistles, the "Testaments of the Twelve Patriarchs," and the Epistle to Diognetus. On the first two subjects, and on "The Silence of Eusebius," connected with the former, I would refer to the very able articles of Professor (now Bishop) Lightfoot in the *Contemporary Review.** As to the Ignatian Epistles, their genuineness in any form is questionable, to say nothing of the state of the text, though the shorter Epistles may belong, in substance, to the middle of the second century; the "Testaments of the Twelve Patriarchs" are interpolated, and need a thoroughly critical edition; and the date of the Epistle to Diognetus is uncertain. In any event, I do not think the references to the Gospel of John in these writings are of great importance.

But to return to our proper subject. The use of the Gospel of John by the Gnostic sects, in the second century, affords a strong, it may seem decisive, argument for its genuineness. However ingeniously they might pervert its meaning, it is obvious to every intelligent reader that this Gospel is, in reality, diametrically opposed to the essential principles of Gnosticism. The Christian Fathers, in their contests with the Gnostics, found it an armory of weapons. Such being the case, let us suppose it to have been forged about the middle of the second century, in the heat of the Gnostic controversy. It was thus a book which the founders of the Gnostic sects, who flourished ten, twenty, or thirty years before, had never heard of. How is it possible, then, to explain the fact that their followers should have not only received it, but have received it, so far as appears, without question or discussion? It must have been received by the

* *Contemporary Review*, January, 1875, xxv. 169 ff., "The Silence of Eusebius"; May, 1875, p. 827 ff., "Polycarp of Smyrna"; August and October, 1875, xxvi. 377 ff., 828 ff., 'Papias of Hierapolis.'' On "the silence of Eusebius," see also Westcott, *Canon of the N. T.*, 4th ed., p. 229 f. With Lightfoot's article in the *Contemp. Review* for February, 1875, "The Ignatian Epistles," should be compared the Preface to *Supernatural Religion*, in the sixth and later editions of that work.

founders of these sects from the beginning; and we have no reason to distrust the testimony of Hippolytus to what is under these circumstances so probable, and is attested by other evidence. But, if received by the founders of these sects, it must have been received at the same time by the catholic Christians. They would not, at a later period, have taken the spurious work from the heretics with whom they were in controversy. It was then generally received, both by Gnostics and their opponents, between the years 120 and 130. What follows? It follows that the Gnostics of that date received it because they could not help it. They would not have admitted the authority of a book which could be reconciled with their doctrines only by the most forced interpretation, if they could have destroyed its authority by denying its genuineness. Its genuineness could then be easily ascertained. Ephesus was one of the principal cities of the Eastern world, the centre of extensive commerce, the metropolis of Asia Minor. Hundreds, if not thousands, of people were living who had known the Apostle John. The question whether he, the beloved disciple, had committed to writing his recollections of his Master's life and teaching, was one of the greatest interest. The fact of the reception of the Fourth Gospel as his work at so early a date, by parties so violently opposed to each other, proves that the evidence of its genuineness was decisive. This argument is further confirmed by the use of the Gospel by the opposing parties in the later Montanistic controversy, and in the disputes about the time of celebrating Easter.

IV. The last external evidence which I shall adduce in favor of the genuineness of the Gospel of John is of a very early date, being attached to the Gospel itself, and found in all the copies which have come down to us, whether in the original or in ancient versions. I refer to what is now numbered as the twenty-fifth verse, with the last half of the twenty-fourth, of the concluding chapter of the Gospel. The last three verses of the chapter read thus: "Hence this report spread among the brethren, that that disciple was not to die; yet Jesus did not say to him that he would not die; but, If I will that he remain till I come, what is that to thee? This is the disciple that testifieth concerning these things, and wrote these things." Here, I suppose, the author of the Gospel ended. The addition follows: "And *we* know that *his* testimony is true. And there are many other things that Jesus did, which, if they should be severally written, *I* do not think that the world itself would contain the books written."

In the words "And *we* know that *his* testimony is true," we manifestly have either a real or a forged attestation to the truth and genuineness of the Gospel. Suppose the Gospel written by an anonymous forger of the middle of the second century: what possible credit could he suppose would be given to it by an anonymous attestation like this? A forger with such a purpose would have named his pretended authority, and have represented the attestation as formally and solemnly given. The attestation, as it stands, clearly presupposes that the author (or authors) of it was known to those who first received the copy of the Gospel containing it.

What view, then, are we to take of it? The following supposition, which I give in the words of Mr. Norton, affords an easy and natural explanation, and, so far as I can see, the only plausible explanation of the phenomena. Mr. Norton says:—

> According to ancient accounts, St. John wrote his Gospel at Ephesus, over the church in which city he presided during the latter part of his long life. It is not improbable that, before his death, its circulation had been confined to the members of that church. Hence copies of it would be afterwards obtained; and the copy provided for transcription was, we may suppose, accompanied by the strong attestation which we now find, given by the church, or the elders of the church, to their full faith in the accounts which it contained, and by the concluding remark, made by the writer of this attestation in his own person.*

The style of this addition, it is further to be observed,

*Norton, *Genuineness of the Gospels*, 2d ed., vol. i., Addit. Notes, p. xcv. f.

differs from that of the writer of the Gospel. It was probably first written a little separate from the text, and afterwards became incorporated with it by a natural mistake of transcribers. According to Tischendorf, the last verse of this Gospel in the Codex Sinaiticus is written in a different hand from the preceding, though by a contemporary scribe. He accordingly rejects it as not having belonged to the Gospel as it was originally written. Tregelles does not agree with him on the palæographical question.

The passage we have been considering suggests various questions and remarks, but cannot be further treated here. I will only refer to the recent commentaries of Godet and Westcott, and end abruptly the present discussion, which has already extended to a far greater length than was originally intended.

Note A. (See p. 24.)

On the quotations of Matt. xi. 27 (*comp.* Luke x. 22) in the writings of the Christian Fathers.

Justin Martyr (*Dial.* c. 100) quotes the following as "written in the Gospel": "All things have been delivered (παραδέδοται) to me by the Father; and no one *knoweth* (γινώσκει) the Father save the Son, neither [knoweth any one] the Son save the Father, and they to whomsoever the Son may reveal him" (οἷς ἂν ὁ υἱὸς ἀποκαλύψῃ). In the *Apology* (c. 63) he quotes the passage twice, thus: "No one *knew* (or "hath known," ἔγνω) the Father save the Son, neither [knoweth any one] the Son save the Father, and they to whomsoever the Son may reveal him"; the order of the words, however, varying in the last clause, in which ὁ υἱός stands once after ἀποκαλύψῃ.

It is unnecessary to quote the corresponding passages in our Gospels in full, as the reader can readily turn to them. The variations of Justin are, (1) the use of the perfect (παραδέδοται), "have been delivered," instead of the aorist (παρεδόθη), strictly, "were delivered," though our idiom often requires the aorist to be translated by the perfect; (2) "*the* Father" for "*my* Father" (omitting μου); (3) the use, in two out of three instances, of the aorist ἔγνω, "knew," or "hath known," instead of the present γινώσκει (this is the word used by Luke; Matthew has ἐπιγινώσκει); (4) the transposition of the two principal clauses; (5) the omission of τις ἐπιγινώσκει, "knoweth any one," in the second clause, if we compare Matthew, or the substitution of "the Father" and "the Son" for "who the Father is" and "who the Son is," if we compare Luke; (6) the use of the plural (οἷς ἂν), "*they* to whomsoever," instead of the singular (ᾧ ἂν), "*he* to whomsoever"; and (7) the substitution of "may reveal" (ἀποκαλύψῃ) for "may will to reveal" (βούληται ἀποκαλύψαι).

The author of *Supernatural Religion* devotes more than ten pages to this passage (vol. i. pp. 401–412, 7th ed.), which he regards as of great importance, and insists, on the ground of these variations, that Justin could not have taken it from our Gospels. To follow him step by step would be tedious. His fundamental error is the assertion that "the peculiar form of the quotation in Justin" (here he refers especially to the variations numbered 3 and 4, above) "occurred in what came to be considered heretical Gospels, and constituted the basis of important Gnostic doctrines" (p. 403). Again, "Here we have the exact quotation twice made by Justin, with the ἔγνω and the same order, set forth as the reading of the Gospels of the Marcosians and other sects, and the highest testimony to their system" (pp. 406, 407). Yet again, "Irenæus states with equal distinctness that Gospels used by Gnostic sects had the reading of Justin" (p. 411). Now Irenæus nowhere states any such thing. Irenæus nowhere speaks, nor does any other ancient writer, of a Gospel of the Marcosians. If this sect had set up a Gospel (*i.e.*, a history of Christ's ministry) of its own, in opposition to the Four Gospels received by the whole Christian Church in the time of Irenæus, we should have had unequivocal evidence of the fact. The denunciations of Marcion for mutilating the Gospel of Luke show how such a work would have been treated. Irenæus is indignant that the Valentinians should give to "a recent work of their own composition" the name of "The Gospel of the Truth" or "The True Gospel" (*Hær.* iii. 11. § 9); but this was in all probability a doctrinal or speculative, not an historical work.* The Valentinians received our four Gospels without controversy, and argued from them in support of their doctrines as best they could. (See Irenæus, *Hær.* i. cc. 7, 8, for numerous examples of their arguments from the Gospels; and compare iii. 11. § 7; 12. § 12; and Tertull. *Præscr.* c. 38.)

Correcting this fundamental error of the author of *Supernatural Religion*, the facts which he himself states respecting the various forms in which this passage is quoted by writers who unquestionably used our four Gospels as their sole or main authority, are sufficient to show the groundlessness of his conclusion. But for the sake of illustrating the freedom of the Christian Fathers in quotation, and the falsity of the premises on which this writer reasons, I will exhibit the facts somewhat more fully than they have been presented elsewhere, though the quotations of this passage have been elaborately discussed by Credner,† Semisch,‡ Hilgenfeld,‖ Volckmar,** and Westcott.†† Of these discussions those by Semisch and Volckmar are particularly valuable.

I will now notice all the variations of Justin from the text of our Gospels in this passage (see above), comparing them with those found in other writers. The two most important (Nos. 3 and 4) will be examined last.

1. παραδέδοται for παρεδόθη is wholly unimportant. It is found in Luke x. 22

* See Norton, *Genuineness of the Gospels*, iii. 227 f.; Westcott, *Canon of the N. T.*, 4th ed., p. 297 f.; Lipsius, art. *Gospels, Apocryphal*, in Smith and Wace's *Dict. of Christian Biog.*, vol. ii. (1880), p. 717.

† *Beiträge zur Einl. in die biblischen Schriften* (1832), i. pp. 248–251.

‡ *Die apostol. Denkwürdigkeiten des Märt. Justinus* (1848), pp. 364–370.

‖ *Kritische Untersuchungen über die Evangelien Justin's*, u. s. w. (1850), pp. 201–206.

** *Das Evang. Marcions* (1852), pp. 75–80. I follow the title in spelling "Volckmar."

†† *Canon of the N. T.*, 4th ed. (1875), pp. 133–135. See also Sanday, *The Gospels in the Second Century*, pp. 132, 133, and chaps. ii., iv., vi.

in the uncial MSS. K and II, the cursives 60, 253, p ^scr^, w ^scr^, three of Colbert's MSS. (see Wetstein *in loc.* and his Prolegom. p. 48), and in HIPPOLYTUS (*Noët.* c. 6), not heretofore noticed.

2. "*The* Father" for "*my* Father," μου being omitted, is equally trivial; so in the Sinaitic MS. and the cursive 71 in Matthew, and in Luke the Codex Bezæ (D), with some of the best MSS. of the Old Latin and Vulgate versions, and other authorities (see Tischendorf), also HIPPOLYTUS as above.

5. The omission of τις ἐπιγινώσκει or its equivalent in the second clause is found in the citation of the MARCOSIANS in Irenæus (i. 20. § 3), other GNOSTICS in Irenæus (iv. 6. § 1), and in IRENÆUS himself three times (ii. 6. § 1; iv. 6. §§ 3, 7, but *not* § 1). It occurs twice in CLEMENT OF ALEXANDRIA (*Pæd.* i. 9, p. 150 ed. Potter; *Strom.* i. 28, p. 425), once in ORIGEN (*Cels.* vi. 17, p. 643), once in ATHANASIUS (*Orat. cont. Arian.* iii. c. 46, p. 596), 6 times in EPIPHANIUS (*Ancor.* c. 67, p. 71, repeated *Hær.* lxxiv. 4, p. 891; c. 73, p. 78, repeated *Hær.* lxxiv. 10, p. 898; and *Hær.* lxiv. 9, p. 643; lxxvi. 7, 29, 32, pp. 943, 977, 981); once in CHRYSOSTOM (*In Joan. Hom.* lx. §1, Opp. viii. 353 (404) A, ed. Montf.), once in PSEUDO-CYRIL (*De Trin.* c. 1), once in MAXIMUS CONFESSOR (*Schol. in* Dion. Areop. *de div. Nom.* c. 1. § 2, in Migne, *Patrol. Gr.* iv. 189), once in JOANNES DAMASCENUS (*De Fide Orth.* i. 1) and twice in GEORGIUS PACHYMERES (*Paraphr. in* Dion. Areop. *de div. Nom.* c. 1, §1, and *de myst. Theol.* c. 5; Migne, iii. 613, 1061). It is noticeable that the CLEMENTINE HOMILIES (xvii. 4; xviii. 4, 13 *bis*, 20) do not here agree with Justin.

6. There is no difference between οἷς ἄν, "*they* to whomsoever," and ᾧ ἄν (or ἐάν), "*he* to whomsoever," so far as the sense is concerned. The plural, which Justin uses, is found in the CLEMENTINE HOMILIES 5 times (xvii. 4; xviii. 4, 13 *bis*, 20), and IRENÆUS 5 times (*Hær.* ii. 6. § 1; iv. 6. §§ 3, 4, 7, and so the Syriac; 7. § 3). The singular is used in the citations given by Irenæus from the MARCOSIANS (i. 20. § 3) and "those who would be wiser than the Apostles," as well as in his own express quotation from Matthew (*Hær.* iv. 6. § 1); and so by the Christian Fathers generally.

7. The next variation (οἷς ἂν ὁ υἱός) ἀποκαλύψῃ for βούληται ἀποκαλύψαι is a natural shortening of the expression, which we find in the citation of the MARCOSIANS (Iren. i. 20. § 3) and in IRENÆUS himself 5 times (ii. 6. § 1; iv. 6. §§ 3, 4, 7, and so the Syriac; 7. § 3); in TERTULLIAN twice (*Marc.* iv. 25; *Præscr.* c. 21), and perhaps in Marcion's mutilated Luke; in CLEMENT OF ALEXANDRIA 5 times (*Cohort.* i. 10, p. 10; *Pæd.* 1. 5, p. 109; *Strom.* i. 28, p. 425; v. 13, p. 697; vii. 18, p. 901; — *Quis dives*, etc., c. 8, p. 939, is a mere allusion); ORIGEN 4 times (*Cels.* vi. 17, p. 643; vii. 44, p. 726; *in Joan.* tom. i. c. 42, p. 45; tom. xxxii. c. 18, p. 450); the SYNOD OF ANTIOCH against Paul of Samosata (Routh, *Rell. sacræ*, ed. alt. iii. 290); EUSEBIUS or MARCELLUS in Eusebius 3 times (*Eccl. Theol.* i. 15, 16, pp. 76 ^c^, 77 ^d^, ἀποκαλύψει; *Ecl. proph.* i. 12 [Migne, *Patrol. Gr.* xxii. col. 1065], ἀποκαλύψῃ); ATHANASIUS 4 or 5 times (*Decret. Nic. Syn.* c. 12, Opp. i. 218 ed. Bened.; *Orat. cont. Arian.* i. c. 12, p. 416; c. 39, p. 443; iii. c. 46, p. 596, in the best MSS.; *Serm. maj. de Fide*, c. 27, in Montf. *Coll. nova*, ii. 14); CYRIL OF JERUSALEM twice (*Cat.* vi. 6; x. 1); EPIPHANIUS 4 times (*Ancor.* c. 67, p. 71, repeated *Hær.* lxxiv. 4, p. 891, but here ἀποκαλύπτει or -τῃ; *Hær.* lxv. 6, p. 613; and without ὁ υἱός, *Hær.* lxxvi. 7, p. 943; c. 29, p. 977); BASIL THE GREAT (*Adv. Eunom.* v. Opp. i. 311 (441) A); CYRIL OF ALEXANDRIA 3 times *Thes.* Opp. v. 131, 149; *Cont. Julian.* viii. Opp. vi. b. p. 270).

All of these variations are obviously unimportant, and natural in quoting from memory, and the extent to which they occur in writers who unquestionably used our Gospels as their sole or main authority shows that their occurrence in Justin affords no ground for supposing that he did not also so use them.

We will then turn our attention to the two variations on which the main stress is laid by the author of *Supernatural Religion*. He greatly exaggerates their importance, and neglects an obvious explanation of their origin.

3. We find ἔγνω, "knew," or "hath known," for γινώσκει or ἐπιγινώσκει, in the CLEMENTINE HOMILIES 6 times (xvii. 4; xviii. 4, 11, 13 *bis*, 20), and once apparently in the RECOGNITIONS (ii. 47, *novit*); twice in TERTULLIAN (*Adv. Marc.* ii. 27; *Præscr.* c. 21); in CLEMENT OF ALEXANDRIA 6 times (*Cohort.* i. 10, p. 10; *Pæd.* i. 5, p. 109; i. 8, p. 142; i. 9, p. 150; *Strom.* i. 28, p. 425; v. 13, p. 697; — once the present, γινώσκει, *Strom.* vii. 18, p. 901; and once, in a mere allusion, ἐπιγινώσκει, *Quis dives*, etc., c. 8, p. 939); ORIGEN uniformly, 10 times (*Opp.* i. 440, 643, 726; ii. 537; iv. 45, 234, 284, 315, 450 *bis*), and in the Latin version of his writings of which the Greek is lost *novit* is used 10 times, including *Opp.* iii. 58, where *novit* is used for Matthew and *scit* for Luke; *scit* occurs also *Opp.* iv. 515. The SYNOD OF ANTIOCH *versus* Paul of Samosata has it once (Routh, *Rell. sacræ*, iii. 290); ALEXANDER OF ALEXANDRIA once (*Epist. ad Alex.* c. 5, Migne, *Patr. Gr.* xviii. 556); EUSEBIUS 6 times (*Eccl. Theol.* i. 12, 16, pp. 72[c], 77[d]; *Dem. Evang.* iv. 3, v. 1, pp. 149[c], 216[d]; *Ecl. proph.* i. 12, Migne xxii. 1065; *Hist. Eccl.* i. 2. § 2); DIDYMUS OF ALEXANDRIA once (*De Trin.* ii. 5, p. 142); EPIPHANIUS twice (*Hær.* lxv. 6, p. 613; lxxiv. 10, p. 898).— Of these writers, Alexander has οἶδε once; Eusebius γινώσκει or ἐπιγινώσκει 3 times, Didymus γινώσκει followed by ἐπιγινώσκει 3 times, Epiphanius has οἶδε 9 or 10 times, and it is found also in Basil, Chrysostom, and Cyril of Alexandria. Marcellus in Eusebius (*Eccl. Theol.* i. 15, 16, pp. 76[c], 78[d]) wavers between οἶδε (twice) and γινώσκει or ἐπιγινώσκει (once), and perhaps ἔγνω (c. 16, p. 77[d]).

4. We find the *transposition* of the clauses, "No one knoweth [*or* knew] the Father" coming first, in one MS. in Matthew (Matthæi's d) and two in Luke (the uncial U and i [scr]), in the *Diatessaron* of TATIAN as its text is given in the Armenian version of Ephraem's Commentary upon it, translated into Latin by Aucher, and published by G. Moesinger (*Evangelii concordantis Expositio*, etc., Venet. 1876),* the CLEMENTINE HOMILIES 5 times (xvii. 4; xviii. 4, 13 *bis*, 20), the MARCOSIANS in Irenæus (i. 20. § 3), other GNOSTICS in Irenæus (iv. 6. § 1), and IRENÆUS himself (ii. 6. § 1; iv. 6. § 3, *versus* § 1 and § 7, *Lat.*, but here a Syriac version represented by a MS. of the 6th century, gives the transposed form; see Harvey's Irenæus, ii. 443), TERTULLIAN once (*Adv. Marc.* iv. 25), ORIGEN once (*De Princip.* ii. 6. § 1, Opp. i. 89, in a Latin version), the SYNOD OF ANTIOCH against Paul of Samosata (as cited above), the MARCIONITE in PSEUDO-ORIG. *Dial. de recta in Deum fide*, sect. i. Opp. i. 817); EUSEBIUS 4 times (*Eccl. Theol.* i. 12; *Dem. Evang.* iv. 3, v. 1; *Hist. Eccl.* i. 2. § 2), ALEXANDER OF ALEXANDRIA once (*Epist. ad Alex.* c. 12, Migne xviii. 565); ATHANASIUS twice (*In illud, Omnia mihi tradita sunt*, c. 5, Opp. i. 107; *Serm. maj. de Fide*, c. 27, in Montf. *Coll. nova*, ii. 14), DIDYMUS once (*De Trin.* i. 26, p. 72), EPIPHANIUS 7 times, or 9 times if the passages transferred from the *Ancoratus* are reckoned (*Opp.* i. 766, 891, 898, 977, 981; ii. 16, 19, 67, 73), CHRYSOSTOM once (*In*

---

* This reads (pp. 117, 216), "Nemo novit Patrem nisi Filius, et nemo novit Filium nisi Pater."

Ascens., etc., c. 14, Opp. iii. 771 (931) ed. Montf.), PSEUDO-CYRIL OF ALEXANDRIA once (*De Trin.* c. 1, Opp. vi. c. p. 1), PSEUDO-CAESARIUS twice (*Dial.* i. *resp.* 3 and 20, in Migne xxxviii. 861, 877), MAXIMUS CONFESSOR once (*Schol. in* Dion. Areop. *de div. Nom.* c. 1. §2, in Migne iv. 189), JOANNES DAMASCENUS once (*De Fide Orth.* i. 1), and GEORGIUS PACHYMERES once (*Paraphr. in* Dion. Areop. *de div. Nom.* c. 1. §1, in Migne iii. 613).

This transposition is found in MS. b of the Old Latin, and some of the Latin Fathers, *e.g.*, Phæbadius (*Cont. Arian.* c. 10); and most MSS. of the Old Latin, and the Vulgate, read *novit* in Matthew instead of *scit* or *cognoscit*, which they have in Luke; but it is not worth while to explore this territory here.

It is manifest from this presentation of the facts that the variations to which the author of *Supernatural Religion* attaches so much importance,— the transposition of the clauses, and the use of the past tense for the present,— being not peculiar to Justin and the heretics, but found in a multitude of the Christian Fathers, can afford no proof or presumption that the source of his quotation was not our present Gospels — that he does not use in making it (*Dial.* c. 100) the term "the Gospel" in the same sense in which it is used by his later contemporaries. It indeed seems probable that the reading ἔγνω, though not in the MSS. which have come down to us, had already found its way into some MSS. of the second century, particularly in Matthew. Its almost uniform occurrence in the numerous citations of the passage by Clement of Alexandria and Origen, and the reading of the Old Latin MSS. and of the Vulgate, favor this view. The transposition of the clauses may also have been found in some MSS. of that date, as we even now find its existence in several manuscripts. But it is not necessary to suppose this; the Fathers, in quoting, make such transpositions with great freedom. The stress laid on the transposition in *Supernatural Religion* is very extravagant. It did not affect the sense, but merely made more prominent the knowledge and the revelation of the Father by Christ. The importance of the change from the present tense to the past is also preposterously exaggerated. It merely expressed more distinctly what the present implied. Further, these variations admit of an easy explanation. In preaching Christianity to unbelievers, special emphasis would be laid on the fact that Christ had come to give men a true knowledge of God, of God in his paternal character. The transposition of the clauses in quoting this striking passage, which must have been often quoted, would thus be very natural; and so would be the change from the present tense to the past. The Gnostics, moreover, regarding the God of the Old Testament as an inferior and imperfect being, maintained that the true God, the Supreme, had been wholly unknown to men before he was revealed by Christ. They would, therefore, naturally quote the passage in the same way; and the variation at an early period would become wide-spread. That Irenæus should notice a difference between the form in which the Gnostics quoted the text and that which he found in his own copy of the Gospels is not strange; but there is nothing in what he says which implies that it was anything more than a various reading or corruption of the text of Matthew or Luke; he nowhere charges the Gnostics with taking it from Gospels peculiar to themselves. It is their *interpretation* of the passage rather than their text which he combats. The change of order further occurs frequently in writers who are treating of the divinity of Christ, as Athanasius, Didymus, Epiphanius. Here the occasion seems to have been that the fact that Christ alone fully knew the

Father was regarded as proving his deity, and the transposition of the clauses gave special prominence to that fact. Another occasion was the circumstance that when the Father and the Son are mentioned together in the New Testament, the name of the Father commonly stands first; and the transposition was the more natural in the present case, because, as Semisch remarks, the word "Father" immediately precedes.

In this statement, I have only exhibited those variations in the quotation of this text by the Fathers which correspond with those of Justin. These give a very inadequate idea of the extraordinary variety of forms in which the passage appears. I will simply observe, by way of specimen, that, while Eusebius quotes the passage at least eleven times, none of his quotations verbally agree. (See *Cont. Marcel.* i. 1, p. 6[a]; *Eccl. Theol.* i. 12, 15, 16 *bis*, 20, pp. 72[c], 76[c], 77[d], 78[a], 88[d]; *Dem. Evang.* iv. 3, v. 1, pp. 149[c], 216[d]; *Comm. in Ps.* cx.; *Ecl. proph.* i. 12; *Hist. Eccl.* i. 2. § 2.) The two quotations which he introduces from Marcellus (*Eccl. Theol.* i. 15 and 16) present a still different form. In three of Eusebius's quotations for εἰ μὴ ὁ πατὴρ he reads εἰ μὴ ὁ μόνος γεννήσας αὐτὸν πατὴρ (*Eccl. Theol.* i. 12, p. 72[c]; *Dem. Evang.* iv. 3, p. 149[c]; and *Hist. Eccl.* i. 2. § 2). If this were found in Justin Martyr, it would be insisted that it must have come from some apocryphal Gospel, and the triple recurrence would be thought to prove it.* The variations in Epiphanius, who also quotes the passage eleven times (not counting the transfers from the *Ancoratus*), are perhaps equally remarkable. PSEUDO-CÆSARIUS quotes it thus (*Dial.* i. *resp.* 3): Οὐδεὶς γὰρ οἶδε τὸν πατέρα εἰ μὴ ὁ υἱός, οὐδὲ τὸν υἱόν τις ἐπίσταται εἰ μὴ ὁ πατήρ. But the false premises from which the author of *Supernatural Religion* reasons have been sufficiently illustrated.

This Note is too long to allow the discussion of some points which need a fuller treatment. I will only call attention to the fact that in the list of passages *in our Gospels* which Irenæus (i. 20. § 2) represents the Marcosians as perverting, there is one which presents a difficulty, and which some have supposed to be taken from an apocryphal Gospel. As it stands, the text is corrupt, and the passage makes no sense. Mr. Norton in the *first edition* of his *Genuineness of the Gospels* (1837), vol. i. Addit. Notes, p. ccxlii., has given a plausible conjectural emendation of the text in Irenæus, which serves to clear up the difficulty. For the πολλάκις ἐπεθύμησα of Irenæus he would read πολλοὶ καὶ ἐπεθύμησαν, for δεῖν, εἶναι (so the old Latin version), and for διὰ τοῦ ἑνός, διὰ τοῦ ἐροῦντος. The passage then becomes a modification of Matt. xiii. 17. Dr. Westcott (*Canon of the N. T.*, 4th ed., p. 306) proposes ἐπεθύμησαν for ἐπεθύμησα, without being aware that his conjecture had been anticipated. But that change alone does not restore sense to the passage. The masterly review of Credner's hypothesis that Justin's Memoirs were the so-called "Gospel according to Peter," which contains Mr. Norton's emendation to which I have referred, was not reprinted in the *second* edition of his work. It seemed to me, therefore, worth while to notice it here.

---

* Compare *Supernatural Religion*, i. 341.

NOTE B. (See p. 25.)

ON THE TITLE, "MEMOIRS BY *the* APOSTLES."

In regard to the use of the article here, it may be well to notice the points made by Hilgenfeld, perhaps the ablest and the fairest of the German critics who regard some apocryphal Gospel or Gospels as the chief source of Justin's quotations. His book is certainly the most valuable which has appeared on that side of the question.*

In the important passage (*Dial.* c. 103), in which Justin says, "In the Memoirs which I affirm to have been composed by the Apostles of Christ and their companions (*ἅ φημι ὑπὸ τῶν ἀποστόλων αὐτοῦ καὶ τῶν ἐκείνοις παρακολουθησάντων συντετάχθαι*), it is written that sweat, like drops of blood [*or* "clots," *θρόμβοι*], flowed from him while he was praying" (comp. Luke xxii. 44), and which Semisch very naturally compares, as regards its description of the Gospels, with a striking passage of Tertullian,† Hilgenfeld insists —

(1) That the article denotes "the collective body" (*die Gesammtheit*) of the Apostles and their companions.

(2) "The Memoirs by the Apostles" is the phrase generally used by Justin. This might indeed be justified by the fact that the Gospels of Mark and Luke were regarded as founded on the direct communications of Apostles or sanctioned by them; but this, Hilgenfeld says, is giving up the sharp distinction between the Gospels as written two of them by Apostles and two by Apostolic men.

(3) The fact that Justin appeals to the "Memoirs by the *Apostles*" for incidents, like the visit of the Magi, which are recorded by only *one* apostle, "shows clearly the utter indefiniteness of this form of expression." ‡ "Manifestly, that single passage," namely, the one quoted above (*Dial.* c. 103), "must be explained in accordance with Justin's general use of language."

Let us examine these points. As to (1), the supposition that Justin conceived of his "Memoirs" as "composed" or "written" — these are the words he uses — by "the collective body" of the Apostles of Christ and "the collective body" of their companions is a simple absurdity.

(2) and (3). For Justin's purpose, it was important, and it was sufficient, to represent the "Memoirs" to which he appealed as resting on the authority of the Apostles. But in one place he has described them more particularly; and it is simply reasonable to say that the more general expression should be interpreted in accordance with the precise description, and not, as Hilgenfeld strangely contends, the reverse.

---

* See his *Kritische Untersuchungen über die Evangelien Justin's, der clementinischen Homilien und Marcion's* (Halle, 1850), p. 13 ff.

† *Adv. Marc.* iv. 2: Constituimus inprimis evangelicum instrumentum apostolos auctores habere. . . . Si et apostolicos, non tamen solos, sed cum apostolis et post apostolos. . . . Denique nobis fidem ex apostolis Ioannes et Matthæus insinuant, ex apostolicis Lucas et Marcus instaurant.

‡ Hilgenfeld also refers to Justin (*Dial.* c. 101, p. 328, comp. *Apol.* i. 38) for a passage relating to the mocking of Christ at the crucifixion, which Justin, referring to the "Memoirs," describes "in a form," as he conceives, "essentially differing from all our canonical Gospels." To me it appears that the agreement is essential, and the difference of slight importance and easily explained; but to discuss the matter here would be out of place, and would carry us too far.

(3) The fact that Justin appeals to the "Memoirs by the Apostles" for an incident which is related by only *one* Apostle is readily explained by the fact that he gives this title to the Gospels considered *collectively*, just as he once designates them as εὐαγγέλια, "Gospels," and twice as τὸ εὐαγγέλιον, "the Gospel." The usage of the Christian Fathers in quoting is entirely analogous. They constantly cite passages as contained "in the Gospels" which are found only in *one* Gospel, simply because "the Gospels" was a term used interchangeably with "the Gospel," to denote the four Gospels conceived of as one book. For examples of this use of the plural, see the note to p. 24. To the instances there given, many might easily be added.

Hilgenfeld, in support of his view of the article here, cites the language of Justin where, in speaking of the new birth, he says, "And the reason for this we have learned from *the* Apostles" (*Apol.* i. 61). Here it seems to me not improbable that Justin had in mind the language of Christ as recorded by the Apostles John and Matthew in John iii. 6, 7, and Matt. xviii. 3, 4. That he had *no* particular Apostles or apostolic writings in view—that by "the Apostles" he meant vaguely "the collective body of the Apostles" does not appear likely. The statement must have been founded on something which he had read *somewhere*.

NOTE C. (See p. 80.)

JUSTIN MARTYR AND THE "GOSPEL ACCORDING TO THE HEBREWS."

After remarking that the "Gospel according to the Hebrews" was "almost universally regarded in the first centuries as the Hebrew original of our canonical Gospel of St. Matthew," that Greek versions of it "must have existed at a very early date," and that "at various times and in different circles it took very different shapes," Lipsius observes: "The fragments preserved in the Greek by Epiphanius betray very clearly their dependence on our canonical Gospels. . . . The Aramaic fragments also contain much that can be explained and understood only on the hypothesis that it is a recasting of the canonical text. . . . The narrative of our Lord's baptism (Epiphan. *Hær.* xxx. 13), with its *threefold* voice from heaven, is evidently a more recent combination of older texts, of which the first is found in the Gospels of St. Mark and St. Luke; the second in the text of the Cambridge *Cod. Bezæ* at St. Luke iii. 22, in Justin Martyr (*Dial. c. Tryphon.* 88, 103), and Clemens Alexandrinus (*Pædag.* i. 6, p. 113, Potter); the third in our canonical Gospel of St. Matthew. And this very narrative may suffice to prove that the so-called 'Hebrew' text preserved by St. Jerome is by no means preferable to that of our canonical Gospel of St. Matthew, and even less original than the Greek text quoted by Epiphanius."* "The attempt to prove that Justin Martyr and the Clementine Homilies had one extra-canonical

---

* Smith and Wace's *Dict. of Christian Biog.*, vol. ii. (1880), p. 710. Many illustrations are here given of the fact that most of the quotations which have come down to us from the "Gospel of the Hebrews" belong to a later period, and represent a later stage of theological development, than our canonical Gospels. Mangold agrees with Lipsius. See the note in his edition of Bleek's *Einleitung in das N. T.*, 3e Aufl. (1875), p. 132 f. Dr. E. A. Abbott, art. *Gospels* in the ninth ed. of the Encyclopædia Britannica (x. 818, note), takes the same view. He finds no evidence that Justin Martyr made any use of the Gospel according to the Hebrews.

authority common to them both, either in the *Gospel of the Hebrews* or in the *Gospel of St. Peter*, . . . has altogether failed. It is only in the rarest cases that they literally agree in their deviations from the text of our Gospels; they differ in their citations as much, for the most part, one from the other as they do from the text of the synoptical evangelists, even in such cases when one or the other repeatedly quotes the same passage, and each time in the same words. Only in very few cases is the derivation from the *Gospel of the Hebrews* probable, as in the saying concerning the new birth (Justin M. *Apol.* i. 61; Clem. *Homilies*, xi. 26; *Recogn.* vi. 9); . . . in most cases . . . it is quite enough to assume that the quotations were made from memory, and so account for the involuntary confusion of evangelic texts." (*Ibid.* p. 712.)

Mr. E. B. Nicholson, in his elaborate work on the Gospel according to the Hebrews (Lond. 1879), comes to the conclusion that "there are no proofs that Justin used the Gospel according to the Hebrews at all" (p. 135). He also observes, "There is no reason to suppose that the authorship of the Gospel according to the Hebrews was attributed to the Apostles generally in the 2d or even the 3d cent. Irenæus calls it simply 'that Gospel which is according to Matthew'" (p. 134).

Holtzmann in the eighth volume of Bunsen's *Bibelwerk* (1866) discusses at length the subject of apocryphal Gospels. He comes to the conclusion that the "Gospel of the Hebrews" or "of the Nazarenes" was an Aramaic redaction (*Bearbeitung*) of our Matthew, executed in an exclusively Jewish-Christian spirit, making some use of Jewish-Christian traditions, but presupposing the Synoptic and the Pauline literature. It was probably made in Palestine for the Jewish-Christian churches some time in the second century (p. 547). The Gospel of the Ebionites, for our knowledge of which we have to depend almost wholly on Epiphanius, a very untrustworthy writer, Holtzmann regards as "a Greek recasting (*Ueberarbeitung*) of the Synoptic Gospels, with peculiar Jewish-Christian traditions and theosophic additions" (p. 553).

Professor Drummond, using Kirchhofer's *Quellensammlung*, has compared the twenty-two fragments of the Gospel according to the Hebrews there collected (including those of the Gospel of the Ebionites) with Justin's citations from or references to the Gospels, of which he finds about one hundred and seventy. I give his result: —

"With an apparent exception to be noticed presently, not one of the twenty-two quotations from the lost Gospel is found among these one hundred and seventy. But this is not all. While thirteen deal with matters not referred to in Justin, nine admit of comparison; and in these nine instances not only does Justin omit everything that is characteristic of the Hebrew Gospel, but in some points he distinctly differs from it, and agrees with the canonical Gospels. There is an apparent exception. Justin quotes the voice from heaven at the baptism in this form, 'Thou art my son; this day have I begotten thee.' 'This day have I begotten thee' is also in the Ebionite Gospel;* but there it is awkwardly appended to a second saying, thus: 'Thou art my beloved Son; in thee was I well pleased; and again, This day have I begotten thee'; — so that the passage is quite different from Justin's, and has the appearance of being a later patchwork. Justin's form of quotation is still the reading of the Codex

* See Epiphanius, *Hær.* xxx. 13; Nicholson, *The Gospel according to the Hebrews*, p. 40 ff. — E. A.

Bezæ in Luke, and, according to Augustine, was found in good MSS., though it was said not to be in the older ones. (See Tischend. in loco.)* One other passage is appealed to. Justin says that, when Jesus *went down upon the water*, a fire was kindled in the Jordan,—*πῦρ ἀνήφθη ἐν τῷ Ἰορδάνῃ*. The Ebionite Gospel relates that, when Jesus *came up from the water*, immediately a great light shone round the place,—*εὐθὺς περιέλαμψε τὸν τόπον φῶς μέγα.* This fact is, I believe, the main proof that Justin used the Gospel according to the Hebrews, and that we may therefore have recourse to it, whenever he differs verbally from the existing Gospels. Considering that the events recorded are not the same, that they are said to have happened at different times, and that the two quotations do not agree with one another in a single word, this argument cannot be considered very convincing, even by those who do not require perfect verbal accuracy in order to identify a quotation. But, further, the author of the anonymous Liber de Rebaptismate says that this event was related in an heretical work entitled Pauli Prædicatio, and that it was not found in any Gospel: 'Item cum baptizaretur, ignem super aquam esse visum; quod in evangelio nullo est scriptum.' (Routh, Rel. Sac. v. pp. 325, 326 [c. 14, Routh; c. 17, Hartel.]) Of course the latter statement may refer only to the canonical Gospels."† To this it may be added that a comparison of the fuller collection of fragments of "the Gospel according to the Hebrews" given by Hilgenfeld or Nicholson (the latter makes out a list of thirty-three fragments) would be still less favorable to the supposition that Justin made use of this Gospel.

In the quotations which I have given from these independent writers, I have not attempted to set forth in full their views of the relation of the original Hebrew Gospel to our Greek Matthew, still less my own; but enough has been said to show how little evidence there is that the "Gospel of the Hebrews" in one form or another either constituted Justin's "Memoirs," or was the principal source from which he drew his knowledge of the life of Christ. While I find nothing like *proof* that Justin made use of any apocryphal Gospel, the question whether he may in a few instances have done so is wholly unimportant. Such a use would not in his case, any more than in that of the later Fathers, as Clement of Alexandria, Origen, Jerome, imply that he placed such a work on a level with our four Gospels.

The notion that Justin used mainly the "Gospel according to Peter," which is assumed, absolutely without evidence, to have been a form of the "Gospel according to the Hebrews," rests almost wholly on the hypothesis, for which there is also not a particle of evidence, that this Gospel was mainly used by the

---

* It is the reading also (in Luke iii. 22) of the best MSS. of the old Latin version or versions, of Clement of Alexandria, Methodius, Lactantius, Juvencus, Hilary of Poitiers in several places, Hilary the deacon (if he is the author of *Quæstiones Vet. et Nov. Test.*), and Faustus the Manichæan; and Augustine quotes it once without remark. It seems to be presupposed in the Apostolical Constitutions (ii. 32); see the note of Cotelier *in loc.* It is altogether probable therefore that Justin found it in his MS. of Luke. The words (from Ps. ii. 7) being repeatedly applied to Christ in the N.T. (Acts xiii. 33; Heb. i. 5; v. 5), the substitution might easily occur through confusion of memory, or from the words having been noted in the margin of MSS. —E. A.

† *Theol. Review*, October, 1875, xii. 482 f., note. The *Liber de Rebaptismate* is usually published with the works of Cyprian.

author of the Clementine Homilies. The agreement between certain quotations of Justin and those found in the Clementine Homilies in their variations from the text of our Gospels is supposed to prove that Justin and Clement drew from a common source; namely, this "Gospel according to Peter," from which they are then imagined to have derived the great body of their citations. The facts stated in the quotation I have given above from Lipsius, who has expressed himself none too strongly, are enough to show the baselessness of this hypothesis; but it may be well to say a few words about the alleged agreement in *five* quotations between Justin and the Clementines in their variations from the text of our Gospels. These are all that have been or can be adduced in argument with the least plausibility. The two most remarkable of them, namely, Matt. xi. 27 (par. with Luke x. 22) and John iii. 3–5, have already been fully discussed.* In two of the three remaining cases, an examination of the various readings in Tischendorf's last critical edition of the Greek Testament (1869–72), and of the parallels in the Christian Fathers cited by Semisch and others, will show at once the utter worthlessness of the argument.†

The last example alone requires remark. This is Matt. xxv. 41, "Depart from me, accursed, into the eternal fire, which is prepared for the devil and his angels." This is quoted by Justin as follows: "Go ye into the outer darkness, which the Father prepared for Satan and his angels." (*Dial.* c. 76.) The Clementine Homilies (xix. 2) agrees with Justin, except that it reads "the devil" for "Satan."

Let us examine the variations from the text of Matthew, and see whether they justify the conclusion that the quotations were taken from a different Gospel.

The first is the substitution of ὑπάγετε, which I have rendered "Go ye," for πορεύεσθε, translated in the common version "depart." The two words, however, differ much less, as they are used in Greek, than *go* and *depart* in English. The common rendering of both is "go." We have here merely the substitution of one synonymous word for another, which is very frequent in quotations from memory. Tischendorf cites for the reading ὑπάγετε here the Sinaitic MS. and HIPPOLYTUS (*De Antichr.* c. 65); so ORIGEN on Rom. viii. 38 in Cramer's *Catena* (p.156) referred to in the *Addenda* to Tregelles's Greek Test.; to which may be added DIDYMUS (*Adv. Manich.* c. 13, Migne xxxix. 1104), ASTERIUS (*Orat.* ii. *in Ps.* v., Migne xl. 412), THEODORET (*In Ps.* lxi. 13, M. lxxx. 1336), and BASIL OF SELEUCIA (*Orat.* xl. § 2, M. lxxxv. 461). Chrysostom in quoting the passage substitutes ἀπέλθετε for πορεύεσθε eight times (*Opp.* i. 27^b ed. Montf.; 285^c; v. 256^e; xi. 29^c; 674^f; 695^d; xii. 291^b; 727^c); and so Epiphanius once (*Hær.* lxvi. 80, p. 700), and Pseudo-Cæsarius (*Dial.* iii. *resp.* 140, Migne xxxviii. 1061). In the Latin Fathers we find *discedite*, *ite*, *abite*, and *recedite*.

---

*See, for the former, Note A; for the latter, p. 31 ff.

†The two cases are (*a*) Matt. xix. 16–18 (par. Mark x. 17 ff.; Luke xviii. 18 ff.) compared with Justin, *Dial.* c. 101, and *Apol.* i. 16, and Clem. Hom. xviii. 1, 3 (comp. iii. 57; xvii. 4). Here Justin's two quotations differ widely from each other, and neither agrees closely with the Clementines. (*b*) Matt. v. 34, 37, compared with Justin, *Apol.* i. 16; Clem. Hom. iii. 55; xix. 2; also James v. 12, where see Tischendorf's note. Here the variation is natural, of slight importance, and paralleled in Clement of Alexandria and Epiphanius. On (*a*) see Semisch, p. 371 ff.; Hilgenfeld, p. 220 ff.; Westcott, *Canon*, p. 153 f.; on (*b*) Semisch, p. 375 f.; Hilgenfeld, p. 175 f.; Westcott, p. 152 f.; Sanday, p. 122 f.

The second variation consists in the omission of *ἀπ' ἐμοῦ*, "from me," and (*οἱ*) *κατηραμένοι*, "(ye) accursed." This is of no account whatever, being a natural abridgment of the quotation, and very common in the citations of the passage by the Fathers; Chrysostom, for example, omits the "from me" fifteen times, the "accursed" thirteen times, and both together ten times (*Opp.* i. 103[d]; v. 191[c]; 473[d]; vii. 296[a]; 571[d]; viii. 356[d]; ix. 679[a]; 709[c]; x. 138[b]). The omission is still more frequent in the very numerous quotations of Augustine.

The third and most remarkable variation is the substitution of *τὸ σκότος τὸ ἐξώτερον*, "the outer darkness," or "the darkness without," for *τὸ πῦρ τὸ αἰώνιον*, "the eternal fire." The critical editors give no various reading here in addition to the quotations of Justin and the Clementines, except that of the cursive MS. No. 40 (collated by Wetstein), which has, as first written, *τὸ πῦρ τὸ ἐξώτερον*, "the *outer* fire," for "the *eternal* fire." It has not been observed, I believe, that this singular reading appears in a quotation of the passage by Chrysostom (*Ad Theodor. lapsum*, i. 9), according to the text of Morel's edition, supported by at least two MSS. (See Montfaucon's note in his edition of Chrysost. *Opp.* i. 11.) This, as the more difficult reading, may be the true one, though Savile and Montfaucon adopt instead *αἰώνιον*, "eternal," on the authority of four MSS.* But it does not appear to have been noticed that CHRYSOSTOM in two quotations of this passage substitutes the "outer darkness" for "the eternal fire." So *De Virg.* c. 24, Opp. i. 285 (349)[e], *ἀπέλθετε γάρ, φησίν, ἀπ' ἐμοῦ εἰς τὸ σκότος τὸ ἐξώτερον τὸ ἡτοιμασμένον κ. τ. λ.* Again, *De Pœnit.* vii. 6, Opp. ii. 339 (399)[b], *πορεύεσθε, οἱ κατηραμένοι, εἰς τὸ σκότος τὸ ἐξώτερον κ. τ. λ.* We find the same reading in BASIL THE GREAT, *Hom. in Luc.* xii. 18, Opp. ii. 50 (70)[d]; in THEODORE OF MOPSUESTIA in a Syriac translation (*Fragmenta Syriaca*, ed. E. Sachau, Lips. 1869, p. 12, or p. 19 of the Syriac), "discedite a me in *tenebras exteriores* quæ paratæ sunt diabolo ejusque angelis"; in THEODORET (*In Ps.* lxi. 13, Migne lxxx. 1336), who quotes the passage in connection with vv. 32–34 as follows: "Go ye (*ὑπάγετε*) into the *outer darkness*, where is the loud crying and gnashing of teeth"; † in BASIL OF SELEUCIA substantially (*Orat.* xl. § 2, M. lxxxv. 461), *ὑπάγετε εἰς τὸ σκότος τὸ ἔ ξ ω, τὸ ἡτοιμασμένον κ. τ. λ.*, and in "SIMEON CIONITA," *i.e.* Symeon Stylites the younger (*Serm.* xxi. c. 2, in Mai's *Nova Patrum Biblioth.* tom. viii. (1871), pars iii. p. 104), "Depart, ye accursed, into the *outer darkness;* there shall be the wailing and gnashing of teeth." ‡ Compare SULPICIUS SEVERUS, *Epist.* i. *ad Sororem*, c. 7: "Ite in *tenebras exteriores*, ubi erit fletus et stridor dentium" (Migne xx. 227[a]). See also Antonius Magnus, Abbas, *Epist.* xx. (Migne, *Patrol. Gr.* xl. 1058), "Recedite a me, maledicti, in ignem æternum, ubi est fletus et stridor dentium."

The use of the expression "the outer darkness" in Matt. viii. 12, xxii. 13, and especially xxv. 30, in connection with "the wailing and gnashing of teeth," and the combination of the latter also with "the furnace of fire" in Matt. xiii. 42, 50, would naturally lead to such a confusion and intermixture of different passages in quoting from memory, or quoting freely, as we see in these

---

* Since the above was written, I have noticed this reading in Ephraem Syrus, *Opp. Gr.* ii. 218[b], *πορεύεσθε ἀπ' ἐμοῦ πάντες οἱ κατηραμένοι εἰς τὸ πῦρ τὸ ἐξώτερον*; and a little below, *πορ. ἀπ' ἐμοῦ οἱ κατηραμένοι εἰς τὸ πῦρ τὸ ἐξώτερον καὶ αἰώνιον, τὸ ἡτοιμασμένον τῷ διαβόλῳ καὶ τοῖς ἀγγέλοις αὐτοῦ.*—*Ibid.* p. 21[8d]. But on pp. 198, 256, 278, 382, 402, Ephraem quotes the passage as it stands in the *textus receptus*. See also Philippus Solitarius, *Dioptra Rei Christianæ*, iv. 20 (Migne, *Patrol. Gr.* cxxvii. 875, b c): "Abite a me procul, longe, maledicti, *in ignem exteriorem*, qui præparatus est diabolo et angelis ejus."

† The last clause reads *ὅπου ὁ βρυγμὸς καὶ ὁ ὀλολυγμὸς τῶν ὀδόντων*, but the words *βρυγμός* and *ὀλολυγμός* seem to have been transposed through the mistake of a scribe.

‡ Simeon Cionita uses the expression *τὸ ἐξώτερον πῦρ*, "the outer fire." *Serm.* xxi. c. 1.

examples. Semisch quotes a passage from Clement of Alexandria (*Quis dives*, etc., c. 13, p. 942), in which Jesus is represented as threatening "fire *and the outer darkness*" to those who should not feed the hungry, etc. Cyril of Alexandria associates the two thus: "What *darkness* shall fall upon them . . . when he shall say, Depart from me, ye accursed, into *the eternal fire*," etc. (*Hom. div.* Opp. v. pars ii. b, p. 408 f.* The fire was conceived of as burning without light. In the case of Justin there was a particular reason for the confusion of the "fire" and the "outer darkness" from the fact that he had just before quoted Matt. viii. 12, as well as the fact that "the outer darkness" is mentioned likewise in the same chapter of Matthew (xxv. 30) from which his quotation is derived (*Dial.* c. 76).

Justin's substitution of "Satan" for "the devil" is obviously unimportant. It occurs in the Jerusalem Syriac and Æthiopic versions, and was natural in the dialogue with Trypho the *Jew*.

The remaining coincidence between Justin and the Clementines in their variation from Matthew consists in the substitution of ὃ ἡτοίμασεν ὁ πατήρ, "which *the Father* prepared" (comp. ver. 34), for τὸ ἡτοιμασμένον, "which is [*or* hath been] prepared." This is of no weight, as it is merely an early various reading which Justin doubtless found in his text of Matthew. It still appears, usually as "*my* Father" for "*the* Father," in important ancient authorities, as the *Codex Bezæ* (D), the valuable cursives 1. and 22., the principal MSS. of the Old Latin version or versions (second century), in IRENÆUS four or five times ("pater," *Hær.* ii. 7. § 3; "pater meus," iii. 23. § 3; iv. 33. § 11; 40. § 2; v. 27. § 1, allus.), ORIGEN in an old Latin version four times (*Opp.* i. 87b, allusion; ii. 177f; 298d; iii. 885c), CYPRIAN three times, JUVENCUS, HILARY three times, GAUDENTIUS once, AUGUSTINE, LEO MAGNUS, and the author of *De Promissis*,—for the references to these, see Sabatier; also in PHILASTRIUS (*Hær.* 114), SULPICIUS SEVERUS (*Ep.* ii. *ad Sororem*, c. 7, Migne xx. 231c), FASTIDIUS (*De Vit. Chr.* cc. 10, 13, M. l. 393, 399), EVAGRIUS presbyter (*Consult.* etc. iii. 9, M. xx. 1164), SALVIAN (*Adv. Avar.* ii. 11; x. 4; M. liii. 201, 251), and other Latin Fathers—but the reader shall be spared.—Clement of Alexandria in an allusion to this passage (*Cohort.* c. 9, p. 69) has "which the *Lord* prepared"; Origen (*Lat.*) reads six times "which *God* prepared" (*Opp.* ii. 161e; 346a; 416f; 431d; 466b; and iv. b. p. 48a, ap. Pamphili *Apol.*); and we find the same reading in Tertullian, Gaudentius, Jerome (*In Isa.* l. 11), and Paulinus Nolanus. Alcimus Avitus has *Deus Pater.*—Hippolytus (*De Antichr.* c. 65) *adds* "which *my Father* prepared" to the ordinary text.

It is clear, I think, from the facts which have been presented, that there is no ground for the conclusion that Justin has here quoted an apocryphal Gospel. His variations from the common text of Matthew are easily explained, and we find them all in the quotations of the later Christian Fathers.

In the exhibition of the various readings of this passage, I have ventured to go a little beyond what was absolutely necessary for my immediate purpose, partly because the critical editions of the Greek Testament represent the patristic authorities so incompletely, but principally because it seemed desirable to expose still more fully the false assumption of *Supernatural Religion* and other writers in their reasoning about the quotations of Justin.

But to return to our main topic. We have seen that there is no *direct* evi-

---

* Comp. Ephraem Syrus, *De Judicio*, Opp. Gr. iii. 402 e f: *οἷον σκότος ἐπιπέσεται ἐπ' αὐτοὺς ὅταν λαλήσει πρὸς αὐτοὺς ἐν ὀργῇ αὐτοῦ, καὶ ἐν τῷ θυμῷ αὐτοῦ πατάξει αὐτοὺς λέγων, πορεύεσθε κ.τ.λ.* (as in the received text). So iii. 97a.

dence of any weight that Justin used either the "Gospel according to the Hebrews" (so far as this was distinguished from the Gospel according to Matthew) or the "Gospel according to Peter." That he should have taken either of these as the source of his quotations, or that either of these constituted the "Memoirs" read generally in public worship in the Christian churches of his time, is in the highest degree improbable. The "Gospel according to the Hebrews" was the Gospel exclusively used by the Ebionites or Jewish Christians; and neither Justin nor the majority of Christians in his time were Ebionites. The "Gospel according to Peter" favored the opinions of the Docetæ; but neither Justin nor the generality of Christians were Docetists. Still less can be said in behalf of the hypothesis that any other apocryphal "Gospel" of which we know anything constituted the "Memoirs" which he cites, if they were one book, or was included among them, if they were several. We must, then, either admit that Justin's "Memoirs" were our four Gospels, a supposition which, I believe, fully explains all the phenomena, or resort to Thoma's hypothesis of an "X-Gospel," *i.e.*, a Gospel of which we know nothing. The only conditions which this "X-Gospel" will then have to fulfil will be: It must have contained an account of the life and teaching of Christ which Justin and the Christians of his time believed to have been "composed by the Apostles and their companions"; it must have been received accordingly as a sacred book, of the highest authority, read in churches on the Lord's day with the writings of the Old Testament prophets; and, almost immediately after he wrote, it must have mysteriously disappeared and fallen into oblivion, leaving no trace behind.*

* Compare Norton, *Genuineness of the Gospels*, 1st ed. (1837), vol. i. pp. 225-230; 2d ed., i. 231 f.

I. INDEX OF NAMES, TOPICS, AND GREEK WORDS.

II. INDEX OF BIBLICAL PASSAGES.

[N.B.— For references of a general character, see the names of the Biblical writers, Mount, Sermon on the, etc., in the preceding index.]

II.

INTERNAL TOKENS OF AUTHORSHIP IN THE FOURTH GOSPEL.

BY ANDREW P. PEABODY.

II.

INTERNAL TOKENS OF AUTHORSHIP IN THE FOURTH GOSPEL.

It is a little singular that, while the Fourth Gospel is of late so largely the subject of controversy, there is no book of the New Testament as to the authorship of which there is a more absolute unanimity among early Christian writers, and, I might say, almost down to our own time; and so far as external evidence is concerned, while a penumbra necessarily rests on the records of what seemed at the outset an obscure provincial sect, that penumbra is, on the whole, less dense on the Fourth Gospel than on the Synoptic Gospels. On the other hand, the chief reasons which have led to the belief that all the Gospels were of post-apostolic origin apply with peculiar force to the Fourth Gospel. These reasons can be best met, if at all, by the contents of the book. If John wrote it, he must have left in it some tokens of his authorship; and it is to these, or to what I so regard, that I now ask your attention.

Ezra Abbot told me, shortly before his death, that it had been his purpose and hope to write a treatise on the internal evidence of the Johannean authorship of the Fourth Gospel. I cannot begin to bend his bow; but I propose to make the best use possible of my own with the same aim.

Of course, no one supposes that John wrote the last two verses; yet there is no proof that the Gospel ever appeared without them. If John wrote the book, it passed into circulation immediately after his death, and the postscript was added by some admiring disciple, who had listened so often and to such a wonderful diversity and wealth of stories about Jesus as to suggest the harmless hyperbole, "If the beloved disciple had written all he knew, he would have made more books than the world could hold." The postscript has the air of being honestly written by a simple-hearted man, rather than by one who wanted to give the book an authority which it could not rightfully claim.

It is of no small evidential significance that John's name does not once occur in the Fourth Gospel. No one doubts that he is often mentioned under the title which it was his supreme joy to bear and own. But no one save himself could have omitted his name. If the Gospel was written in good faith, but not by John, the writer, who gives a great many names — more names of apostles than occur in all the Synoptics together, except in the lists of the sacred college — would certainly have told who the beloved apostle was; and, if the book was written with the purpose of passing it off as John's, his name would have been paraded as often as possible in the Gospel itself, and would never have been omitted in the postscript. But it was very natural for John himself to merge his own personality in the most blessed privilege that ever man had,— especially as that title has by no means the stately formality which it conveys to the modern ear; but, had it been written in the English which had not then begun to be, it would have been expressed by the phrase "his most intimate friend," or simply "his friend," the singular number supplying the needed emphasis.

The narrative immediately preceding the postscript could have been written by no one but John. It is designed to account for a rumor that Jesus had foretold that John would live to the end of the world, which the disciples supposed to be very near,— and we have no proof that Jesus himself may not have thought so; for he expressly says that he does not know. I do not suppose that the conversation here given had any spiritual meaning, or would have been remembered or recorded but for the mistake that grew from it. Let me give my rendering of the story. Seven of the apostles went a-fishing. On landing they found preparations in progress by their friends on shore for a simple meal. Jesus was there. When they had eaten, he addressed himself to Peter, giving him his apostolic charge, and intimating the mode by which in dying he would seal his life-testimony. Jesus had arranged with John to stay on or near the spot, and at the same time had something which he wished to communicate in private to Peter. He asked Peter to follow him. The other disciples, all but John, were getting their fishing gear ready to go. Peter turned, and saw John, not in the group, but standing just behind his Master and himself. Peter asked, "Why does he stay here, instead of going with his brother and the rest of them?" Jesus replied, "Why need it give you any concern, if I have asked him to stay till we return?" He was overheard, perhaps only in part, by the other disciples; such words as they caught they not unnaturally connected with the profoundly solemn subjects on which he had no doubt been talking with them as with Peter; and they imagined that by "staying till I come back" he meant "living till my second coming." Any seeming harshness in our Saviour's words to Peter may be accounted for by the difficulty of representing Syro-Chaldaic colloquialisms in a language of which the writer had not a free command. Now I cannot believe that any person but John would have had this explanation in mind, would have thought of giving it, or have known how to give it. Especially strange would it have been that so trivial a matter should have lasted on to the latter part of the second century, to which many critics relegate the authorship of the Fourth Gospel.

The almost uniform tradition is that John lived during his last years at Ephesus, and lived to a great old age. I think that we shall find in the Fourth Gospel abundant evidence that it was written by a native of Judæa, by a Hebrew then living remote from Palestine, by a resident of Ephesus before, or not long after, the close of the first Christian century, by a person familiarly conversant with the events recorded, and by an old man.

That the author was familiar with Judæa is evident. There is a singular minuteness of local detail and description which could have been authentic only if written by one conversant with places, customs, festivals, and observances, and which no outsider could have so counterfeited as to escape easy detection.

At the same time there constantly occur explanations which no Hebrew could have needed, such as the minute description of the pool of Bethesda, the mention of the passover as "a feast of the Jews," of "the Jews' feast of tabernacles," of Bethsaida and Cana as in Galilee, of Bethany as "about fifteen furlongs from Jerusalem," of the sea or lake of Galilee as the sea of Tiberias, the name by which it was known outside of Palestine. There is also the interpretation of Hebrew words, familiar to every Jewish ear, as of Messiah, Cephas, Siloam, even Rabbi (elsewhere used in the New Testament without interpretation) and Rabboni. In the Synoptic Gospels there are but three seeming instances of interpretation, and these not by any means similar to those which I have just specified, but cases in which the Syro-Chaldaic words are interpolated, evidently on account of the intense impression made by their utterance. All three of these are in Mark's Gospel, of which, not by tradition alone, but by many internal tokens, we may account Peter as virtually the author, Mark as little else than the amanuensis. The instances are "Talitha-cumi," "Ephphatha," and "Eloi, Eloi, lama sabachthani," which undoubtedly fell on Peter's ear with so strong an ictus that he never could repeat either of these narratives or suffer them to be written without inserting the *ipsissima verba*. The last of these utterances reappears in the Greek of Matthew's Gospel, copied probably from Mark.

That the Fourth Gospel was written among Gentiles may be seen also in its perpetual use of the term *Jews* (Ἰουδαῖοι), the term by which Gentile writers of that period always designated the Hebrews,—a term, indeed, not unfamiliar in Judæa, but employed by the Synoptics only in a single instance, except as used by or with special reference to Pilate or

Roman officials, and thus as a Gentile rather than a Hebrew designation.

The Fourth Gospel could hardly have been written anywhere but at Ephesus. The proem evidently refers to an incipient Gnosticism of the type traditionally identified with Cerinthus, with whom John's encounter at the bath may have been a myth, yet one which could hardly have found currency, had not the two men been at Ephesus at the same time. Irenæus expressly says that there was in this Gospel special reference to the heresies of Cerinthus; but if, as is alleged by a certain class of critics, Irenæus was credulous enough to accept as more than half a century old a book written late in his lifetime, we of course can lay no stress on his testimony; yet he has commonly been regarded as trustworthy in his statements of fact. Now the most authentic account of Cerinthus is that he was a Jew or Jewish proselyte of Alexandria, and that in Asia Minor he incorporated Philo's doctrine of the Logos with the angelology which was going to give birth to the unnumbered æons of more advanced Gnosticism. The Alexandrian conception, or at least one type of it, was that of a creative Logos, distinct from and inferior to the Supreme Being. This our author deals with at the outset, identifying the Logos with God. In the third verse αὐτοῦ refers grammatically, and, I believe, in the author's intention to God (Θεόν), not to the Logos (ὁ λόγος), so that the meaning of the passage is, "All things were created by God," not by any separate creative Logos, διὰ (*by* or *through*) with the genitive not infrequently denoting the efficient cause. But, if the more usual interpretation be maintained, the sense would still be the same, so far as the negation of an independent creative power is concerned; for διὰ with the genitive is familiarly used to denote an instrumental or secondary cause, the sense in that case being, "God was the Creator; the Logos, but the instrument." But, as I interpret the passage, the Logos is not referred to after the second till the fourteenth verse, where the writer speaks of the incarnation of the Logos, the communicable, all of God that can be made flesh and can assume a human form. Ζωὴ (life) and Φῶς (light) were among the earliest of the Gnostic æons, and our Gospel denies their existence as separate spiritual essences, and maintains that Light flows from God, to kindle in man all of life that is worth living. This proem makes me believe that the Gospel was written at Ephesus.

The same considerations induce me to assign to the Gospel no later date than is consistent with the hypothesis that John wrote it. In taking cognizance of Gnosticism, it would, of course, have made strictures on that of its own time. But early in the second century there was an outblooming of theories far wilder and more fantastic than any that had been ascribed to Cerinthus. Basilides and Valentinus had, in their respective creeds, each a pantheon of spiritual essences or æons more densely peopled than Olympus at its fullest; and the Ophites, along with other absurdities, gave a prominent place among their virtual demigods to the serpent who

> "Brought death into the world, and all our woes,
> With loss of Eden."

Now the author of the proem of the Fourth Gospel could not have left these vagaries unnoticed, had they been rife when he wrote; and in a subsequent portion of the Gospel he could hardly have made reverent mention of the brazen serpent without an irreverent word for the older serpent that had been restored to favor by the posterity of their victimized ancestress.

The Fourth Gospel must also, of necessity, antedate the apocryphal gospels, some of which can be traced back to the earlier part of the second century. These writings show the sort of myth that was growing up out of the tradition of the Christ,—the silly stories of prodigies, sometimes contemptibly trivial, sometimes wickedly malicious, that passed current among converts, it may be, to Christian piety, but not to common sense or rational discernment. The most sceptical must admit that, if God in man ever transcended the accustomed course of events, the cases of the kind recorded in the Fourth Gospel are credible; while we can conceive of him as permitting the marvellous events narrated in the apocryphal gospels, only by supposing that for the time he abdicated the portion of the godhead comprehended under the attributes of perfect wisdom and holiness. Indeed, the conception of Christ, the (so called) miracles included, in the Fourth Gospel, bears a very close kinship to that in the confessedly genuine Epistles of Paul, which must have been written considerably before the close of the first century.

There is another not unimportant consideration that forbids our assigning a later date than John's lifetime for the Fourth Gospel. The capacity of authorship in the early Christian Church was amazingly slender and feeble. The remains, both genuine and spurious, of the (so called) Apostolic Fathers, are harmlessly pietistic, but have not force of thought or style sufficient to have kept them alive if they had been written at a later date. We have to go down to the fourth century, to the time of Chrysostom and Augustine, before we find any Christian writer whom it would not be absurd to regard as capable, even with the help of the Synoptic Gospels, of putting together such discourses as those in the Fourth Gospel. If there had been in the second century a man capable of such writing, his name would not have been lost, even with the misleading postscript. Indeed, he could not have wanted to conceal his name. No man could write thus, and not let the world know it, unless he were consciously the reporter of one immeasurably his superior, which John may have been, but which no volunteer gospel-writer of the second century can have been.

In the next place, the very minute circumstantiality of the Fourth Gospel goes far toward making me believe without a doubt that it was written by some one who was conversant with the scenes and events described. Though so much of it is taken up with long discourses, there is tenfold more of detail in it than in the Synoptics. The writer not only names more than half of the apostles, but introduces some of them several times, and tells what they said and did, how and when. Similar mention is made of several other persons. The Synoptic Gospels contain hardly any collateral matter, except such as is necessary in putting on record what our Saviour said and did; while the Fourth Gospel contains a great deal that is not essential to the story, though adding largely to its interest.

The character of the Synoptic Gospels in this respect is easily accounted for. The apostles were together at Jerusalem for several weeks after their Master had left them, and their main employment would naturally have been to refresh one another's memory as to what he had done, and especially as to the very words which had fallen from his lips. Thus there grew up an oral gospel, which was virtually the basis of the Synoptic Gospels. Of these, Matthew's, in the vernacular, may or may not have been the oldest. Mark's was the oldest written in Greek. The translator of Matthew's Gospel used it. It was the principal of Luke's authorities, though he had access to a portion of our Saviour's ministry not recorded by the others. It seems to me very probable that this portion covers the period when the twelve were absent on their short missionary tour. He may have been one of the seventy, whose call is named by him alone, and he may have been with Jesus while the apostles were absent. In support of this hypothesis, I lay no stress on the occurrence of his name in some old lists of the seventy; but I do lay great stress on his intimate knowledge of what took place on the walk to Emmaus. He must have known who was with Cleopas on that walk, and he certainly would have named him, had it been any other than himself. This by way of parenthesis. What I want to say is that the oral gospel from which the Synoptics grew was, by the very nature of the case, limited in its scope. The author of the Fourth Gospel had no such limitation. He also probably had a scope entirely outside of theirs. He describes several journeys to and sojourns in or near Jerusalem of which they may have known nothing. When Jesus did not have the twelve with him, he would have been likely to take one of them as his companion, and that one was probably the writer of this Gospel. The reason why I think so is that, while we have in the Fourth Gospel many long discourses, even these are broken up by frequent interlocutions, and their occasions are described with a painstaking accuracy, which, if not authentic, seems only the more entirely so on the closest scrutiny, and indicates an inventive faculty unsurpassed, if not unequalled.

I would next say that in the Fourth Gospel there are unmistakable tokens of senility, which accord with the tradition that John wrote it in his late old age. I am well fitted to speak on this point. There is something marvellous in an old man's memory. The back-setting of its current troubles the waters all the way up, and brings to the surface, oh! so many things that in earlier life seemed sunk never to rise. It is a blessed thing and a subject for devout gratitude that, when one begins to find himself alone and a stranger in the rapidly rushing present, there is this inevitable return to the long past on which the morning sunbeams shine again. We undoubtedly forget much that is recent; but of this we are not aware except when a needless officiousness reminds us of it. But it is wonderful how long-forgotten scenes and events recur, with petty details that make them as fresh as if they were of yesterday. I can recall a great deal more of my childhood, youth, and early manhood than I could ten years ago. I can live over again scenes that had been for three-fourths of my lifetime in entire oblivion. I can bring up in thought processions of small events in their precise order, with circumstances too insignificant to be worth recalling except as they make the picture more vivid. I can tell how things looked, how people dressed, what they talked about, the precise spot where such and such trivial incidents took place or were told to me.

Now I see numerous traces of such an old man's memory in the Fourth Gospel. If John wrote it, it is by no means what it would have been if he had written it at sixty, or even at seventy years of age. Among the tokens that the writer of this Gospel saw and heard what he wrote, many are such as a man in middle life would not have called to remembrance or thought of specifying. The very first chapter gives a series of interviews of four disciples with one another, with John the Baptist, and with Jesus, having a somewhat confused appearance to a hasty reader, and containing in seventeen verses not more than five that have any bearing on the main object of the story, while two more would have sufficed for the explanation of the five. The story in its minute and complicated details unrolls itself and straightens itself out, as such a narrative does in an old man's mind, in a way that adds a charm to what is really interesting, while it is the secret of the tediousness of narrative to which we old men are fearfully liable.

The account of the marriage in Cana is given in the same way. We have the by-play of conversation both before and after the miracle, the number and the ordinary use of the stone jars, and a rough estimate of how much they held. We are thankful for such sections of the life going on about our Saviour, and thankful that there was with him a man who grew old enough to sketch them as a younger man would not have done.

The narrative of the Samaritan visit has its interest greatly enhanced by the accumulation of details really unessential, but to us very precious. We have Christ's weariness with the long morning's walk, his sitting by the well which with its site is carefully described, the hour of his arrival, the mission of some of the party to buy food for the rest, then the woman with five husbands, and the sixth ready to take, or already extra-legally filling the place left vacant by her last divorce, the return of the disciples, and then what the woman said to her friends and they to her. The great spiritual lessons of that visit occupy about a sixth part of the narrative, and would be amply explained by another sixth; and Mark would have comprehended in ten verses what our author tells in forty-two, not one of which, however, would we be willing to spare.

The same particularity of narration, with whatever inference may be drawn from it, will be seen in many portions of the Gospel, some of which I shall specify, which are so intensely realistic in their details as to demonstrate their own authenticity, whoever put them on record, and which, it seems to me, could have been written only by one personally conversant with them, and some of them only by an old man.

Under this head I will ask your attention, first, to the case of the man born blind. I never knew in actual life a more real, genuine character than his. He is said to have been a street-beggar, and well known. What sort of a person would a blind beggar be in one of our quiet, stationary, not over-crowded towns or cities? He would be treated good-naturedly, but not respectfully. The street *gamins* would chaff him, and make fun of him; and many older persons, especially when they put their small coins into his wallet, would discharge at him their harmless volleys of coarse wit. His own wit would be sharpened by theirs. He would give as he received. He would in every such encounter be quick in appropriate rejoinder. He would be no respecter of persons, but would have a ready answer, and that almost always a smart repartee, for whatever was said to him, by gentle or simple. Now this blind man is just such a person. He has not had the use of his eyes long enough to stand in awe of the Pharisees. They cannot get round him. He chaffs them unmercifully. Divest his language of the stilted form of our translation, and you have precisely the way in which such a man would talk now. "I know nothing about his being a sinner,—that's no concern of mine. But there's one thing that I do know,—I was blind, and I have got my eyesight." They return to the charge, and he answers, "I've told you the whole story once, and you wouldn't believe it. What do you mean by wanting me to go over it again? Are you going to be his disciples?" Then again, and his reply, when they say, "We know not whence he is," has a very sharp sting,—"It's something very strange, isn't it? that somebody that you don't know about should have made me see." They find that they can do nothing with him, and therefore set the example so faithfully followed by Christian Pharisees of a later date, of excommunicating the man who will not yield to them. This man is painted to the life. He must have told the story himself, what the Pharisees said to him and what he said to them; and it is manifestly rehearsed in the Fourth Gospel by one who enjoyed it and was greatly amused by it at the time, and took pleasure in recalling it years and years afterward.

Another and very different self-authenticating narrative, which could have been written only by an eye-witness, is the raising of Lazarus. Here, again, the story is minutely circumstantial,—the talk with and of his disciples on the way, the sisters, as, one after the other, they meet Jesus, the friendly and the hostile Jews, the successive stages of the procession graveward, the sympathy, the tears, the prayer, the voice that wakes the dead. The whole story is as natural as it is sublime. He who wrote it must have been there. It transcends, not only the power of fiction, but the possibility of narration at second-hand. There are in it traits that could not have been transmitted by hearsay. That utterance to Martha, those divinest words ever spoken on earth, were in their tender simplicity just what she needed to hear, and it is not for any sonorous grandeur that fits them for august ceremonial use, but because they flow with heavenly consolation into the believing mourner's heart and soul, that we repeat them now when dust returns to dust, and that they will echo from grave to grave till the last of the dying shall have put on immortality. There is no page in history which, as we read, so distinctly paints itself on the retina of the inward vision. As we move on with the sorrowing sisters in that divine companionship, the shadow of death lifts itself and rolls away; majestic sweetness and sovereign love have attained their climax before we reach the tomb; and nothing seems more natural than that the dead should hear that voice, and live.

I have named these as instances in which the writer must have been an eye and ear witness. This is equally true, and equally authentic are the tokens of an old man's memory, in the description of the last supper, of the events of the following night and day, and of the resurrection. My limits will not permit me to enter into all the details which I should be glad to present as they impress me in reading them. But I will name two or three portions of the narrative which deserve special comment.

The washing of the disciples' feet is given in the Fourth Gospel alone, and it is described circumstantially, as it could not have been by hearsay or at second-hand, but only by one who was present, or by a practised and accomplished writer of fiction who had trained himself to give perfect verisimilitude to the creations of his own brain.

The giving of the sop to Judas is peculiar to the Fourth Gospel. According to Mark, Jesus says to the twelve that one of the twelve that dip with him in the dish — the dish of bitter-sweet sauce in which they all dipped their bread — should betray him; but he does not designate the traitor; for they, one by one, ask, "Is it I?" After this statement, according to the Fourth Gospel, Peter beckons to John to ask Jesus who the traitor is. John, reclining on the bosom of Jesus, asks him in a whisper or in a low voice, and Jesus replies, addressing him alone, "It is the man to whom I shall offer this sop, or piece of bread, when I have dipped it." John, therefore, knows what the others did not know till several hours afterward. They suppose that Judas goes out on some business connected with the feast. No one but John could have written this incident, which is not so much as hinted at by the Synoptics, and was probably not within their cognizance; for we may suppose that even Peter failed to hear Christ's answer to John's question.

One incident more. Christ's committing his mother to John's care was undoubtedly known to all the apostles; but, as it was not mentioned by either of the Synoptics, it would have been strange that it should have been invented, or fished up from unwritten tradition, by some unknown gospel-writer in the middle or later part of the second century; while John could not have helped writing it.

I am only giving instalments of what to my mind makes up all the narrative portions of the Fourth Gospel. The more closely I study it, the more strongly am I convinced that it is a first-hand narrative. I do not like to speak confidently of such a thing as the critical sense, so much must there always be in it of the personal equation. But, of the four Gospels, those of Matthew and Luke read to me like an oft-repeated story written down. In that of Mark, I can detect the Petrine element, and only Peter could have given the precise account that we have there of his denial of his Master; and yet I can see how his words flowed with somewhat less freedom and fervor from another's pen than they would from his own. But in the Fourth Gospel I feel sure that the eyes which saw, the ears that heard, and the hand that wrote belonged to the same man; and, if so, that man must have been John.

There are yet two objections to the Johannean authorship of the Fourth Gospel, which I ought not to overlook. One relates to the character of the discourses there recorded. They differ widely in substance and in style from those in the Synoptic Gospels. They have the air of elaborate compositions, like the speeches which the Greek and Roman historians put into the mouths of their heroes.

As to the difference of substance or material in the first three Gospels and the Fourth, it must be borne in mind that in several instances the audiences were of a very different type. At Jerusalem Jesus had to encounter a skilled subtilty of argument, which needed to be confronted by a logic on its own intellectual plane, while in a higher spiritual sphere. That some of the discourses of this sort were given substantially as they were uttered, would appear from the frequency with which those who are addressed interpose their objections and cavils, which never fail of an appropriate reply. Then as to what was uttered to Galilean audiences and in the hearing of the other apostles, it is conceivable that John had a spiritual receptivity which they had not, so that there sank deep into his heart much which only glanced over their heads. Then, too, if he was at times the sole companion, as well as the closest friend, of his Master, much that the others heard and remembered but imperfectly may have been talked over with him in private, and thus have obtained an enduring lodgment in his memory.

But that John, if John it was, exercised the function of an editor no less than that of a chronicler, I have no doubt. I do not suppose that all which is reported without break was said continuously. I can easily believe that the writer abridged, amplified, arranged, compiled, according to his best judgment; and that, if John was the writer, his presentation of what his Master said may have often taken the shape which it had assumed in his habitual method of preaching, in which he would naturally have brought together utterances on different occasions, connected in his mind by likeness of subject or by some other law of association.

Then, too, John may have intentionally adopted the method of his time, and often wrought detached sayings or sentiments of his Master into discourses of which the form was his own, the spirit Christ's, and the words, too, in great part, the translation of his. We do not know that John may not, while at Ephesus, have become conversant with classic models of biography and history. He and his brother probably held a higher social position than the other apostles. His father owned his fishing vessel, and hired his crew. In our New England fishing towns this would have indicated a certain aristocracy of rank. How much it meant in Galilee we cannot tell. But Zebedee's wife or widow seems to have made much of it when she claimed for her sons the chief places in the kingdom that was to be, and James, as the foremost victim of Herod's murderous spite, evidently held in the church at Jerusalem the primacy, which afterward devolved on his namesake. Then, if John was the "disciple known unto the high priest," and so well known that he could take the liberty of bringing Peter into the palace, he must have had a social standing somewhat different from that of his fellow-disciples. Now, if this was the case, he not improbably was better educated than they, and thus capable, as they might not have been, of appreciating and copying such methods of historical composition as might easily have become familiar to him during his residence in what was virtually a Grecian city. I have no doubt that the portion of the Fourth Gospel from the fourteenth to the seventeenth chapter (inclusive) contains much that was not spoken on the night of the betrayal. The fourteenth chapter has in it so much of dialogue that we may regard it as a literal narrative of what Jesus said and of what was said to him during the paschal supper, closing with his words, "Arise, let us go hence." In the two following chapters we have, as I suppose, John's reminiscences of other kindred sayings close under the forecast shadow of the cross. Then the seventeenth chapter embodies, it may be, the spirit and the remembered phraseology of prayers offered on more than one occasion as the end drew near.

But what concerns us is the words themselves, not how they were written. Now if there ever were written words of counsel and comfort, to enlighten, gladden, uplift, sanctify the soul of man, which as truly flow from the throne of God into every heart that will take them in as if they fell on the individual ear from the parted heavens, those words are in this Fourth Gospel. If ever one prayed on earth who, while he prayed, was consciously in the bosom of the Eternal Father, it was he in whose interceding heart we in this distant age and land were not forgotten, when he prayed not for his disciples alone, but for them who should believe on him through their word. Such words as we have in this Gospel can have come from no being below a Christian's conception of Jesus Christ; and they could have been committed to writing only by one, like John, unspeakably near to the heart of Jesus.

It remains only for me to consider the objection to the authorship of the Fourth Gospel by John on account of the (so called) miracles which it records; which, it is said, could not have taken place, and which, therefore, can have been put on record only in a post-apostolic age. This is termed the application of historical criticism to the Gospel in question. It is, however, precisely the reverse of what passes under that title as applied to secular literature. The founder of this school of critics was Niebuhr, who, by the way, professed his belief in the authenticity of the gospel narratives, as he would have been compelled to do by the very canons of criticism that bear his name. He did not say,—"What passes current as Livy's History contains a great deal of fabulous matter; therefore Livy could not have written it." What he said was,—"Livy undoubtedly wrote the History that bears his name, and he is a good witness for whatever came within his knowledge; but he received a great many traditions from questionable sources, and for these his authority is worthless." The Biblical critic who would adopt his method, and yet discredit the Fourth Gospel, would have to say,—"John undoubtedly wrote this Gospel; for all Christian antiquity ascribed it to him, without a particle of opposing evidence. But John is not to be believed. He was the easy dupe of imposture or false appearances, or else he knowingly falsified his testimony; for much of what he records can never have happened." This ground no one could take without stultifying himself. The reasoning therefore is, "The Fourth Gospel describes impossible events, therefore it could not have been written by an eye-witness; but—all evidence to the contrary notwithstanding—it must have been written at least half a century, if not a full century, after John's death."

Now as to these miracles, it is very certain that the greatest of them all, Christ's own resurrection, was believed in John's lifetime; for it is affirmed as an undoubted fact in those of Paul's Epistles which the critics of what deems itself the most advanced school admit to be genuine. Indeed, the confident belief of the apostles in the reality of this event is asserted by Baur, Strauss, and Renan, who all say that, but for this belief, Christianity would have perished in its Founder's tomb. But if the resurrection did not take place, and yet John with his fellow-apostles believed that it did, may not a man so credulous as John must have been have believed the less marvellous events ascribed in the Fourth Gospel to the power of Jesus? I cannot see how the question of miracles affects in the least that of the authorship of the Fourth Gospel, if we suppose all of the sacred college (would not *sacred* be in that case a burlesque misnomer?) to have been so silly as to be duped by a series of optical illusions, started by a case of mistaken identity in the early dawn as Mary Magdalene stood by the sepulchre.

But as to the impossibility of what are called miracles, who dares to affirm this? If there is a God, it is he that does, through the normal sequence of second causes, whatever is done in the universe; and, though this sequence is seldom suspended, it is certainly within his power to arrest it at any point, and it is conceivable that, for the supreme interest and the eternal well-being of his human family, he may have arrested it at some decisive epoch in the history of the world.

But miracle, in the common sense of the word, is not a necessary hypothesis. There are occurring, all along the ages, and never more than now, especially in the realm wrongfully usurped by pseudo-spiritualism, phenomena which we believe to take place in harmony with established natural laws, which yet we cannot begin to explain by those laws, so far as we now understand them. Now, in entire accordance with those same natural laws, may not the one being who, of all that ever trod this earth, has not claimed, but won the "name above every name"; who climbed the summit of moral excellence on which no other son of man has stood, and which none have approached except through the might and love of his spirit,—might not he, I say, by virtue of what he was, have had a command of external nature — nay, of that realm of departed spirits, for aught that we know, lying close around us — which is supernatural only in the sense in which the force which our immeasurably inferior will-power is constantly exerting over nature is supernatural? I am strongly inclined to believe that many of the events which we are wont to regard as miraculous occur under laws of nature which are either wholly unknown to us, or which, though known to us, have a scope far beyond our accustomed experience.

However this may be, I cannot deny the possibility of such events as the Fourth Gospel records till I am so far conscious of omniscience as to know all that it was ever possible for God to do. There is a reverent, devout, truly, though anticipatively Christian agnosticism in that magnificent portion of the Book of Job in which, by the boldest flight of hallowed poetical imagination, God himself speaks, in a voice which every soul of man ought to hear: "Where wast thou when I laid the foundation of the earth? Declare, if thou hast understanding. . . . Have the gates of death been opened unto thee? or hast thou seen the doors of the shadow of death? . . . Where is the way where light dwelleth? and as for darkness, where is the place thereof? . . . Knowest thou it, because thou wast then born? or because the number of thy days is great?"

III.

INTERNAL EVIDENCE FOR THE AUTHENTICITY AND GENUINENESS OF SAINT JOHN'S GOSPEL.

By the late Right Rev. J. B. LIGHTFOOT,
Bishop of Durham.

III.

INTERNAL EVIDENCE FOR THE AUTHENTICITY AND GENUINENESS OF SAINT JOHN'S GOSPEL.

THIS lecture originally formed one of a series connected with Christian evidences, and delivered in St. George's Hall in 1871. The other lectures were published shortly afterwards; but, not having been informed beforehand that publication was expected, I withheld my own from the volume. It seemed to me that in the course of a single lecture I could only touch the fringes of a great subject, and that injustice would be done by such imperfect treatment as alone time and opportunity allowed. Moreover, I was then, and for some terms afterwards, engaged in lecturing on this Gospel at Cambridge, and I entertained the hope that I might be able to deal with the subject less inadequately if I gave myself more time. Happily, it passed into other and better hands, and I was relieved from this care.

A rumor got abroad at the time, and has (I am informed) been since repeated, that I did not allow the lecture to be published because I was *dissatisfied* with it. I was only dissatisfied in the sense which I have already explained. It could not be otherwise than unsatisfactory to bring forward mere fragmentary evidence of an important conclusion, when there was abundant proof in the background. The present publication of the lecture is my answer to this rumor. I give it after eighteen years exactly in the same form in which it was originally written, with the exception of a few verbal alterations. Looking over it again after this long lapse of time, I have nothing to withdraw. Additional study has only strengthened my conviction that this narrative of Saint John could not have been written by any one but an eye-witness.

As I have not dealt with the external evidences except for the sake of supplying a statement of the position of antagonists, the treatment suffers less than it would otherwise have done from not being brought down to date. I have mentioned, by way of illustration, two respects in which later discoveries had falsified Baur's contentions. The last eighteen years would supply several others. I will single out three: (1) The antagonists of the Ignatian Epistles are again put on their defence. The arguments which were adduced against the genuineness of these epistles will hold no longer. Ignatius has the testimony of his friend and contemporary, Polycarp; and Polycarp has the testimony of his own personal disciple, Irenæus. The testimony of Irenæus is denied by no one; the testimony of Polycarp is only denied because it certifies to the Ignatian letters. Before we are prepared to snap this chain of evidence rudely, and to break with an uninterrupted tradition, we require far stronger reasons than have been hitherto adduced. (2) Justin Martyr wrote before or about the middle of the second century. His use of the Fourth Gospel was at one time systematically denied by the impugners of its apostolic authorship. Now it is acknowledged almost universally, even by those who do not allow that this evangelical narrative was written by Saint John himself. (3) The "Diatessaron" of Tatian was written about A.D. 170, and consisted of a "Harmony of Four Gospels." Baur and others contended that, at all events, Saint John was not one of the four. Indeed, how could it be? for it had not been written, or only recently written, at this time. The "Diatessaron" itself has been discovered, and a commentary of Ephrem Syrus upon it in Armenian has likewise been unearthed within the last few years, both showing that it began with the opening words of Saint John.

The fourth of our canonical Gospels has been ascribed by the tradition of the Church to Saint John, the son of Zebedee, the personal disciple of our Lord, and one of the twelve apostles. Till within a century (I might almost say, till within a generation) of the present time, this has been the universal belief — with one single and unimportant exception — of all ages, of all churches, of all sects, of all individuals alike.

This unanimity is the more remarkable in the earlier ages of the Church, because the language of this Gospel has a very intimate bearing on numberless theological controversies which started up in the second, third, and fourth centuries of the Christian era; and it was therefore the direct interest of one party or the other to deny the apostolic authority, if they had any ground for doing so. This happened not once or twice only, but many times. It would be difficult to point to a single heresy promulgated before the close of the fourth century which might not find some imaginary points of coincidence or some real points of conflict — some relations, whether of antagonism or of sympathy — with this Gospel. This was equally true of Montanism in the second century, and of Arianism in the fourth. The Fourth Gospel would necessarily be among the most important authorities — we might fairly say *the* most important authority — in the settlement of the controversy, both from the claims which it made as a product of the beloved apostle himself, and from the striking representations which it gives of our Lord's teaching. The defender or the impugner of this or that theological opinion would have had a direct interest in disproving its genuineness and denying its authority. Can we question that this would have been done again and again if there had been any haze of doubt hanging over its origin,— if the antagonist could have found even a *prima facie* ground for an attack?

And this brings me to speak of that one exception to the universal tradition to which I have already alluded. Once, and once only, did the disputants in a theological controversy yield to the temptation, strong though it must have been. A small, unimportant, nameless sect,— if indeed they were compact enough to form a sect,— in the latter half of the second century, denied that the Gospel and the Apocalypse were written by Saint John. These are the two canonical writings which especially attribute the title of the Word of God, the Logos, to our Lord: the one, in the opening verses, "In the beginning was the Word, and the Word was with God, and the Word was God"; the other, in the vision of Him who rides on the white horse, whose garments are stained with blood, and whose name is given as the "Word of God." To dispose of the doctrine, they discredited the writings. Epiphanius calls them *Alogi*, "the opponents of the Word," or (as it might be translated, for it is capable of a double meaning) "the irrational ones." The name is avowedly his own invention. Indeed, they would scarcely have acknowledged a title which had this double sense and could have been so easily turned against themselves. They appear only to disappear. Beyond one or two casual allusions, they are not mentioned; they have no place in history.

This is just one of those exceptions which strengthen the rule. What these *Alogi* did, numberless other sectaries and heretics would doubtless have done if there had been any sufficient ground for the course. But even these *Alogi* lend no countenance to the views of modern objectors. Modern critics play off the Apocalypse against the Gospel, allowing the genuineness of the former, and using it to impugn the genuineness of the latter. Moreover, there is the greatest difference between the two. The modern antagonist places the composition of the Fourth Gospel in the middle or the latter half of the second century; these ancient heretics ascribed it to the early heresiarch Cerinthus, who lived at the close of the first century, and was a contemporary of Saint John. Living themselves in the latter half of the second century, they knew (as their opponents would have reminded them if they had found it convenient to forget the fact) that the Gospel was not a work of yesterday, that it had already a long history, and that it went back at all events to the latest years of the apostolic age; and in their theory they were obliged to recognize this fact. I need hardly say that the doctrine of the Person of Christ put forward in the Gospel and the Apocalypse is diametrically opposed to the teaching of Cerinthus, as every modern critic would allow. I only allude to this fact to show that these very persons, who form the single exception to the unanimous tradition of all the churches and all the sects alike, are our witnesses for the antiquity of the Gospel (though not for its authenticity), and therefore are witnesses *against* the modern impugners of its genuineness.

With this exception, the early testimony to the authenticity and genuineness of the Gospel is singularly varied. It is a remarkable and an important fact that the most decisive and earliest testimony comes not from Fathers of the orthodox Church, but from heretical writers. I cannot enter upon this question at length, for I did not undertake this afternoon to speak of the *external* evidence; and I ask you to bear in mind that any inadequate and cursory treatment necessarily does a great injustice to a subject like this, for the ultimate effect of testimony must depend on its fulness and variety. I only call attention to the fact that within the last few years most valuable additions have been made to this external testimony, and these from the opposite extremes of the heretical scale. At the one extreme we have *Ebionism*, which was the offspring of Judaizing tendencies; at the other, *Gnosticism*, which took its rise in Gentile license of speculation and practice. Ebionism is represented by a remarkable extant work belonging to the second century, possibly to the first half of the second century, the *Clementine Homilies*. The greater part of this work has long been known; but until within the last few years the printed text was taken from a MS. mutilated at the end, so that of the twenty Homilies the last half of the nineteenth and the whole of the twentieth are wanting. These earlier Homilies contained more than one reference to gospel history which could not well be referred to any of the first three evangelists, and seemed certainly to have been taken from the fourth. Still, the reference was not absolutely certain, and the impugners of Saint John's Gospel availed themselves of this doubt to deny the reference to this Gospel. At length, in the year 1853, Dressel published for the first time, from a Vatican MS., the missing conclusion of these Homilies; and this was found to contain a reference to the incidents attending the healing of the man born blind, related only by Saint John, and related in a way distinctly characteristic of Saint John,— a reference so distinct that no one from that time has attempted to deny or dispute it.

So much for the testimony of Ebionism,— of the *Judaic* sects of early Christianity. But equally definite, and even more full, is the testimony which recent discovery has brought to light on the side of *Gnosticism*. Many of my hearers will remember the interest which was excited a few years ago by the publication of a lost treatise on heresies, which Bunsen and others ascribed (and, as is now generally allowed, correctly ascribed) to Hippolytus, in the earlier part of the third century. This treatise contains large and frequent extracts from previous Gnostic writers of diverse schools,— Ophites, Basilidians, Valentinians; among them, from a work which Hippolytus quotes as the production of Basilides himself, who flourished about A.D. 130–140. And in these extracts are abundant quotations from the Gospel of Saint John.

I have put these two recent accessions to the external testimony in favor of the Fourth Gospel side by side, because, emanating from the most diverse quarters, they have a peculiar value as showing the extensive circulation and wide reception of this Gospel at a very early date; and because also, having been brought to light soon after its genuineness was for the first time seriously impugned, they seem providentially destined to furnish an answer to the objections of recent criticism.

If we ask ourselves why we attribute this or that ancient writing to the author whose name it bears,— why, for instance, we accept this tragedy as a play of Sophocles, or that speech as an oration of Demosthenes,— our answer will be that it bears the name of the author, and (so far as we know) has always been ascribed to him. In very many cases we know nothing, or next to nothing, about the history of the writing in question. In a few instances we are fortunate enough to find a reference to it, or a quotation from it, in some author who lived a century or two later. The cases are exceptionally rare when there is an indisputable allusion in a contemporary, or nearly contemporary, writer. For the most part, we accept the fact of the authorship because it comes to us on the authority of a MS. or MSS. written several centuries after the presumed author lived, supported in some cases by quotations in a late lexicographer or grammarian or collection of extracts.

The external testimony in favor of Saint John's Gospel reaches back much nearer to the writer's own time and is far more extensive than can be produced in the case of most classical writings of the same antiquity. From the character of the work, also, this testimony gains additional value; for where the contents of a book intimately affect the cherished beliefs and the practical conduct of all who receive it, the universality of its reception, amidst jarring creeds and conflicting tendencies, is far more significant than if its contents are indifferent, making no appeal to the religious convictions and claiming no influence over the life. We may be disposed to complain that the external testimony is not so absolutely and finally conclusive in itself that no door is open for hesitation, that all must, despite themselves, accept it, and that any investigation into the internal evidence is superfluous and vain. But this we have no right to demand. If it is as great, and more than as great as would satisfy us in any other case, this should suffice us. In all the most important matters which affect our interests in this world and our hopes hereafter, God has left some place for diversity of opinion, because He would not remove all opportunity of self-discipline.

If, then, the genuineness of this Gospel is supported by greater evidence than in ordinary cases we consider conclusive, we approach the investigation of its internal character with a very strong presumption in its favor. The *onus pro-*

bandi rests with those who would impugn its genuineness, and nothing short of the fullest and most decisive marks of spuriousness can fairly be considered sufficient to counterbalance this evidence.

As I proceed, I hope to make it clear that, allowing their full weight to all the difficulties (and it would be foolish to deny the existence of difficulties) in this Gospel, still the internal marks of authenticity and genuineness are so minute, so varied, so circumstantial, and so unsuspicious as to create an overwhelming body of evidence in its favor.

But, before entering upon this investigation, it may be worth while to inquire whether the hypotheses suggested by those who deny the genuineness of this Gospel are themselves free from all difficulties. For, if it be a fact (as I believe it is) that any alternative which has been proposed introduces greater perplexities than those which it is intended to remove, we are bound (irrespectively of any positive arguments in its favor) to fall back upon the account which is exposed to fewest objections, and which at the same time is supported by a continuous and universal tradition.

We may take our start from Baur's theory; for he was the first to develop and systematize the attack on the genuineness of the Fourth Gospel. According to Baur it was written about the year 170. The external testimony, however, is alone fatal to this very late epoch; for, after all wresting of evidence and post-dating of documents, it is impossible to deny that at this time the Gospel was not only in existence, but also received far and wide as a genuine document; that it was not only quoted occasionally, but had even been commented upon as the actual work of Saint John. Consequently, the tendency of later impugners has been to push the date farther back, and to recede from the extreme position of this, its most determined and ablest antagonist. Hilgenfeld, who may be regarded as the successor of Baur, and the present representative of the Tübingen school (though it has no longer its headquarters at Tübingen), would place its composition about the year 150; and Tayler, who a few years ago (1867) reproduced the argument of

Baur and others in England, is disposed to assign it to about the same date. With a strange inconsistency he suggests, towards the close of his book, that its true author may have been John the presbyter, though John the presbyter is stated by Papias (who had conversed with this John, and from whom all the information we possess respecting him is derived) to have been a personal disciple of our Lord, and therefore could hardly have outlived John the apostle, and certainly could not have been living towards the middle of the second century.

This tendency to recede nearer and nearer to the evangelist's own age shows that the pressure of facts has begun to tell on the theories of antagonistic criticism, and we may look forward to the time when it will be held discreditable to the reputation of any critic for sobriety and judgment to assign to this Gospel any later date than the end of the first century, or the very beginning of the second.

But, meanwhile, let us take the earliest of these dates (A.D. 140) as less encumbered with difficulties, and therefore more favorable to the opponents of its genuineness, and ask whether a gospel written at such a time would probably have presented the phenomena which we actually find in the fourth canonical Gospel. We may interrogate alike its omissions and its contents. On this hypothesis, how are we to account for what it has left unsaid, and for what it has said?

Certainly, it must be regarded as a remarkable phenomenon that on many ecclesiastical questions which then agitated the minds of Christians it is wholly silent, while to others it gives no distinct and authoritative answer. Our Lord's teaching has indeed its bearing on the controversies of the second century, as on those of the fourth, or of the twelfth, or of the sixteenth, or of the nineteenth; but, as in these latter instances, its lessons are inferential rather than direct, they are elicited by painful investigation, they are contained implicitly in our Lord's life and person, they do not lie on the surface, nor do they offer definite solutions of definite difficulties.

Take, for instance, the dispute concerning the episcopate. Contrast the absolute silence of this Gospel respecting this institution with the declarations in the Epistles of Ignatius. A modern defender of the episcopate will appeal to the commission given to the apostles (John xx. 22, 23). I need not stop here to inquire to what extent it favors his views. But, obviously, it is quite insufficient by itself. It would serve almost equally well for an apostolically ordained ministry of any kind, for a presbyterial as for an episcopal succession. Is it possible that a writer, composing a gospel at the very time when the authority of this office had been called in question, if a supporter of the power of the episcopate, would have resisted the temptation of inserting something which would convey a sanction, if an opponent, something which would convey a disparagement, of this office, in our Lord's own name?

Or, again, take the Gnostic theories of emanations. Any one who has studied the history of the second century will know how large a place they occupy in the theological disputes of the day; what grotesque and varied forms they assume in the speculations of different heretical teachers; what diverse arguments, some valid, some fanciful, are urged against them by orthodox writers. Would a forger have hesitated for a moment to slay this many-headed hydra by one well-aimed blow? What can we suppose to have been the object of such a forger, except to advance certain theological views? And why should he have let slip the very opportunity, which (we must suppose) he was making for himself, of condemning the worst forms of heresy from our Lord's own lips? It is true that you and I think we see (and doubtless think rightly) that the doctrine of God the Word taught in Saint John's Gospel is the real answer to the theological questionings which gave rise to all these theories about æons or emanations, and involves implicitly and indirectly the refutation of all such theories. But it is only by more or less abs ruse reasoning that we arrive at this conclusion. The early Gnostics did not see it so: they used Saint John's Gospel, and retained their theories notwithstanding. A forger would have taken care to provide a direct refutation which it was impossible to misunderstand.

Or, again, about the middle of the second century the great controversy respecting the time of celebrating Easter was beginning to lift up its head. For the latter half of this century the feud raged, bursting out ever afresh and disturbing the peace of the Church again and again, until it was finally set at rest in the fourth century at the Council of Nicæa. Was the festival of the Lord's resurrection to be celebrated always on the same day of the week, the Sunday? or was it to be guided by the time of the Jewish Passover, and thus to take place on the same day of the month, irrespective of the day of the week? Each community, each individual, took a side in this controversy.

Unimportant in itself, it seriously endangered the existence of the Church. The daring adventurer who did not hesitate to forge a whole gospel would certainly not be deterred by any scruple from setting the matter at rest by a few strokes of the pen. His narrative furnished more than one favorable opportunity for interposing half a dozen decisive words in our Lord's name; and yet he abstained.

Thus we might take in succession the distinctive ecclesiastical controversies of the second century, and show how the writer of the Fourth Gospel holds aloof from them all,—certainly, a strange and almost incredible fact, if this writer lived about the middle or even in the latter half of the century, and, as a romancer, was not restrained by those obligations of fact which fetter the truthful historian who is himself a contemporary of the events recorded.

But, if the omissions of the writer are strange and unaccountable on the assumption of the later date of the Gospel, the actual contents present still greater difficulties on the same hypothesis. In the interval between the age when the events are recorded to have taken place and the age in which the writer is supposed to have lived, a vast change had come over the civilized world. In no period had the dislocation of Jewish history been so complete. Two successive hurricanes had swept over the land and nation. The devastation of Titus had been succeeded by the devastation of Hadrian. What the locust of the first siege had left the canker-worm of the second had devoured. National polity, religious worship, social institutions, all were gone. The city had been razed, the land laid desolate, the law and the ordinances proscribed, the people swept into captivity or scattered over the face of the earth. "Old things had passed away: all things had become new."

Now let us place ourselves in the position of one who wrote about the middle of the second century, after the later Roman invasion had swept off the scanty gleanings of the past which had been spared from the earlier. Let us ask how a romancer so situated is to make himself acquainted with the incidents, the localities, the buildings, the institutions, the modes of thought and feeling, which belonged to this past age and (as we may almost say) this bygone people. Let it be granted that here and there he might stumble upon a historical fact, that in one or two particulars he might reproduce a national characteristic. More than this would be beyond his reach. For, it will be borne in mind, he would be placed at a great disadvantage, compared with a modern writer; he would have to reconstruct history without those various appliances, maps and plates, chronological tables, books of travel, by which the author of a historical novel is so largely assisted in the present day.

And, even if he had been furnished with all these aids, would he have known how to use them? The uncritical character of the apostolic age is a favorite commonplace with those who impugn the genuineness of the canonical Scriptures or the trustworthiness of the evangelical narratives. I do not deny that the age (compared with our own) was uncritical, though very exaggerated language is often used on the subject. But, obviously, this argument has a double edge. And the keener of these two edges lies across the very throat of recent negative criticism. For it requires a much higher flight of critical genius to invent an extremely delicate fiction than to detect it when invented. The age which could not expose a coarse forgery was incapable of constructing a subtle historical romance. This one thing I hope to make clear in the short time that is allowed me this afternoon. The Fourth Gospel, if a forgery, shows the most consummate skill on the part of the forger; it is (as we should say in modern phrase) thoroughly in keeping. It is replete with historical and geographical details; it is interpenetrated with the Judaic spirit of the time; its delineations of character are remarkably subtle; it is perfectly natural in the progress of the events; the allusions to incidents or localities or modes of thought are introduced in an artless and unconscious way, being closely interwoven with the texture of the narrative; while throughout the author has exercised a silence and a self-restraint about his assumed personality which is without a parallel in ancient forgeries, and which deprives his work of the only motive that, on the supposition of its spuriousness, would account for his undertaking it at all.

In all these respects it forms a direct contrast to the known forgeries of the apostolic or succeeding ages. I will only ask my hearers who are acquainted with early apocryphal literature to compare Saint John's Gospel with two very different and yet equally characteristic products of the first and second centuries of the Christian era,—with the *Protevangelium*, or Gospel of the Infancy of Jesus, on the one hand, and with the *Clementine Homilies*, on the other: the former, a vulgar daub dashed in by a coarse hand in bright and startling colors; the other, a subtle philosophical romance, elaborately drawn by an able and skilful artist. But both the one and the other are obviously artificial in all their traits, and utterly alien to the tone of genuine history.

Such productions as these show what we might expect to find in a gospel written in the middle or after the middle of the second century.

If, then, my description of the Fourth Gospel is not overcharged (and I will endeavor to substantiate it immediately), the supposition that this Gospel was written at this late epoch by a resident at Alexandria or at Ephesus will appear in the highest degree incredible; and, whatever difficulties the traditional belief may involve, they are small indeed, compared with the improbabilities created by the only alternative hypothesis.

I have already proved that the absence of certain topics in this Gospel seems fatal to its late authorship. I shall now proceed to investigate those phenomena of its actual contents which force us to the conclusion that it was written by a Jew contemporary with and cognizant of the facts which he relates, and more especially those indications which fix the authorship on the Apostle Saint John. It is necessary, however, to premise, by way of caution, that exhaustive treatment is impossible in a single lecture, and that I can only hope to indicate a line of investigation which any one may follow out for himself.

First of all, then, the writer was a Jew. This might be inferred with a very high degree of probability from his Greek style alone. It is not ungrammatical Greek, but it is distinctly Greek of one long accustomed to think and speak through the medium of another language. The Greek language is singularly rich in its capabilities of syntactic construction, and it is also well furnished with various connecting particles. The two languages with which a Jew of Palestine would be most familiar,—the Hebrew, which was the language of the sacred Scriptures, and the Aramaic, which was the medium of communication in daily life—being closely allied to each other, stand in direct contrast to the Greek in this respect. There is comparative poverty of inflections, and there is an extreme paucity of connecting and relative particles. Hence in Hebrew and Aramaic there is little or no syntax, properly so called.

Tested by his style, then, the writer was a Jew. Of all the New Testament writings the Fourth Gospel is the most distinctly Hebraic in this respect. The Hebrew simplicity of diction will at once strike the reader. There is an entire absence of periods, for which the Greek language affords such facility. The sentences are co-ordinated, not subordinated. The clauses are strung together, like beads on a string. The very monotony of arrangement, though singularly impressive, is wholly unlike the Greek style of the age.

More especially does the influence of the Hebrew appear in the connecting particles. In this language the single connecting particle ו is used equally, whether co-ordination or opposition is implied; in other words, it represents "but" as well as "and." The Authorized Version does not adequately represent this fact, for our translators have exercised considerable license in varying the renderings: "then," "moreover," "and," "but," etc. Now, it is a noticeable fact that in Saint John's Gospel the capabilities of the Greek language in this respect are most commonly neglected; the writer falls back on the simple "and" of Hebrew diction, using it even where we should expect to find an adversative particle. Thus v. 39, 40, "Ye search the Scriptures, for in them ye think ye have eternal life: *and* they are they which testify of Me: *and* ye will not come to me"; vii. 19, "Did not Moses give you the law, *and* none of you keepeth the law?" where our English version has inserted an adversative particle to assist the sense, "and *yet*"; vii. 30, "Then they sought to take Him: *and* no man laid hands on Him," where the English version substitutes "but no man"; vii. 33, "Then said Jesus unto them, Yet a little while am I with you, *and* I go to Him that sent Me," where again our translators attempt to improve the sense by reading "and *then*." And instances might be multiplied.

The Hebrew character of the diction, moreover, shows itself in other ways,—by the parallelism of the sentences, by the repetition of the same words in different clauses, by the order of the words, by the syntactical constructions, and by individual expressions. Indeed, so completely is this character maintained throughout that there is hardly a sentence which might not be translated literally into Hebrew or Aramaic, without any violence to the language or to the sense.

I might point also to the interpretations of Aramaic words, as Cephas, Gabatha, Golgotha, Messias, Rabboni, Siloam,

Thomas, as indicating knowledge of this language. On such isolated phenomena, however, no great stress can fairly be laid, because such interpretations do not necessarily require an extensive acquaintance with the language; and, when the whole cast and coloring of the diction can be put in evidence, an individual word here and there is valueless in comparison.

There are, however, two examples of proper names in this Gospel on which it may be worth while to remark, because the original is obscured in our English Bibles by a false reading in the Greek text used by our translators, and because they afford incidentally somewhat strong testimony to the writer's knowledge both of the language and of contemporary facts.

The first of these is *Iscariot*. In the other three Gospels this name is attributed to the traitor apostle Judas alone. In Saint John's Gospel also, as represented in the received text and in our English version, this is the case. But if the more correct readings be substituted, on the authority of the ancient copies, we find it sometimes applied to Judas himself (xii. 4, xiii. 2, xiv. 22), and sometimes to Judas's father Simon (*e.g.*, vi. 71, "He spake of Judas the son of Simon Iscariot"; xiii. 26, "He giveth to Judas the son of Simon Iscariot"). Now this shows that the evangelist knew this not to be a proper name, strictly so called, but to describe the native place of the person, "the man of Kerioth," and hence to be applicable to the father and the son alike.

The other instance which I shall give, at first sight presents a difficulty; but, when further investigated, it only adds fresh testimony to the exact knowledge of the Fourth Evangelist. In Saint Matthew, Simon Peter is called Bar-Jona (Matt. xvi. 17); *i.e.*, son of Jona (or Jonan or Jonas). Accordingly, in the received text of Saint John also he appears in not less than four passages (i. 42, xxi. 15–17) as Simon son of Jona (or Jonan or Jonas). But there can be no reasonable doubt that the correct reading in all these four passages is "Simon son of Joannes"—the Hebrew and Aramaic Johanan, the English John—and that later transcribers have altered it to make it accord with the form adopted by Saint Matthew. Here there is an apparent discrepancy, which, however, disappears on examination; for we find that Jona or Jonan or Jonas is more than once used in the LXX. version of the Old Testament as a contracted form of the name Johanan, Johannes, or John. Thus the statements of the two evangelists are reconciled; and we owe it to the special knowledge derived from the Fourth Gospel that the full and correct form is preserved. For, when we have once got this key to the fact, we can no longer question that John was the real name of Peter's father, since it throws great light on our Lord's words in Saint Matthew. The ordinary name Jonah, which was borne by the prophet, and which is generally supposed to be the name of Simon's father, signifies "a dove"; but the name Johanan or John is "the grace of God." Hence the Baptist is called, not Zacharias, as his relatives thought natural, but John, in accordance with the heavenly message (Luke i. 13), because he was specially given to his parents by God's grace. So, too, the call of Saint Peter (John i. 42) becomes full of meaning: "Thou art Simon, the son of the grace of God; thou shalt be called Cephas"; and the final commission given to the same apostle is doubly significant, when we interpret the thrice repeated appeal as "Simon, son of God's grace, lovest thou Me?" for without this interpretation the studied repetition of his patronymic seems somewhat meaningless. Bearing this fact in mind, we turn to the passage of Saint Matthew (xvi. 17): "Jesus answered and said unto him, Blessed art thou, Simon Bar-Jona (son of the grace of God): for flesh and blood hath not revealed it unto thee, but My Father which is in heaven. And I say unto thee, That thou art Peter, and upon this rock I will build My Church." His name and his surname alike are symbols and foreshadowings of God's special favor to him in his call and commission. This is only one of many instances in which the authenticity of the statements of the Fourth Gospel is confirmed by the fact that they incidentally explain what is otherwise unexplained in the narrative of the synoptic evangelists.

Another evidence that the writer was acquainted with the Hebrew language is furnished by the quotations from the Old Testament. This evangelist, like Saint Paul, sometimes cites from the current Greek version of the Seventy, and sometimes translates directly from the Hebrew. When a writer, as is the case in the Epistle to the Hebrews, quotes largely and quotes uniformly from the LXX. version, this is at least an indication that he was not acquainted with the original; and hence we infer that the epistle just mentioned was not written by Saint Paul, a Hebrew of the Hebrews, but by some disciple, a Hellenistic Jew, thoroughly interpenetrated with the apostle's mind and teaching, but ignorant of the language of his forefathers. If on any occasion the quotations of a writer accord with the original Hebrew against the LXX. version, we have a right to infer that he was acquainted with the sacred language,—was, in fact, a Hebrew or Aramaic-speaking Jew. Several decisive examples might be produced, but one must suffice. In xix. 37 is a quotation from Zechariah xii. 10, which in the original is, "They shall look upon Me whom they pierced." Accordingly, it is given in Saint John, "They shall look on him whom they pierced" (ὄψονται εἰς ὃν ἐξεκέντησαν). But the LXX. rendering is, "They shall gaze upon Me, because they insulted" (ἐπιβλέψονται πρός με, ἀνθ' ὧν κατωρχήσαντο), where the LXX. translators had a different reading, רָקְדוּ for דָּקָרוּ, and where their Greek rendering has not a single word in common with Saint John's text.

In xii. 40, again, the evangelist quotes Isaiah vi. 10, "Because that Esaias said again, He hath blinded their eyes, and hardened their heart; that they should not see with their eyes," etc. Now, this quotation is far from being verbally exact; for in the Hebrew the sentence is imperative, "Make fat the heart of this people, and make heavy their ears, and close their eyes, that they should not see with their eyes," etc. Yet, on the other hand, it does not contain any of the characteristic renderings of the LXX.; and this is one distinct proof that, however loosely quoted, it was derived, not from the LXX., but from the original. For the LXX.

translators, taking offence, as it would seem, at ascribing the hardening of the heart to God's own agency, have thrown the sentence into a passive form: "The heart of this people was made fat, and with their ears they heard heavily, and their eyes they closed," etc., so as to remove the difficulty. If, therefore, the evangelist had derived the passage from the LXX., it is inconceivable that he would have reintroduced the active form, thus wantonly reviving a difficulty, unless he had the original before him.

I will only add one other example. In xiii. 18 occurs a quotation from Psalm xli. 9. Here the expression which in the original signifies literally "made great" or "made high" his heel is correctly translated "lifted up his heel" (ἐπῆρεν τὴν πτέρναν αὐτοῦ), as in the A.V. of the Psalms. The LXX. version, however, gives ἐμεγάλυνεν πτερνισμόν. "He multiplied [or increased] tripping up with the heel," or "treachery," which has given rise to the paraphrastic rendering in our Prayer-book version, "laid great wait for me." Here, again, it is obvious that the evangelist's quotation could not have been derived from the LXX., but must have been rendered either directly from the Hebrew or (what for my purpose is equally decisive) indirectly through some Chaldee targum.

If, therefore, we had no other evidence than the language, we might with confidence affirm that this Gospel was not written either by a Gentile or by a Hellenistic Christian, but by a Hebrew accustomed to speak the language of his fathers. This fact alone negatives more than one hypothesis which has been broached of late years respecting its authorship; for it is wholly inconsistent with the strictly Gentile origin which most recent theories assign to it. But, though irreconcilable with Gentile authorship, it is not wholly inconsistent with the later date; for we cannot pronounce it quite impossible that there should be living in Asia Minor or in Egypt, in the middle or after the middle of the second century, a Judaic Christian familiar with the Hebrew or Aramaic language, however rare such instances may have been.

Having thus established the fact that the writer was neither a Gentile nor a Hellenist, but a Hebrew of the Hebrews, we will proceed to inquire further whether he evinces an acquaintance with the manners and feelings, and also with the geography and history (more especially the contemporary history) of Palestine, which, so far as our knowledge goes (and in dealing with such questions we must not advance one step beyond our knowledge), would be morally impossible with even a Hebrew Christian at the supposed date, long after the political existence of the nation had been obliterated, and when the disorganization of Jewish society was complete.

As I am obliged to compress my remarks within the space of a single lecture, I cannot place the evidence fully before you; but my hope is that I may indicate the lines of investigation which will enable you to answer it more completely for yourselves. I will only say that we obtain from the Fourth Gospel details at once fuller and more minute on all these points than from the other three. Whether we turn to the Messianic hopes of the chosen people, with all the attendant circumstances with which imagination had invested this expected event, or to the mutual relations of Samaritans, Jews, Galilæans, Romans, and the respective feelings, prejudices, beliefs, customs of each, or to the topography as well of the city and the temple as of the rural districts — the Lake of Gennesaret, and the corn-fields and mountain ridges of Shechem — or to the contemporary history of the Jewish hierarchy and the Herodian sovereignty, we are alike struck at every turn with subtle and unsuspicious traces, betokening the familiarity with which the writer moves amidst the ever-shifting scenes of his wonderful narrative.

This minuteness of detail in the Fourth Evangelist is very commonly overlooked, because our gaze is arrested by still more important and unique features in this Gospel. The striking character of our Lord's discourses as recorded in Saint John — their length and sequence, their simplicity of language, their fulness and depth of meaning — dazzles the eye of the critic and blinds him to the historical aspects of the narrative. Only by concentrating our view on these latter shall we realize the truth that the evangelist is not floating in the clouds of airy theological speculation, that, though with his eye he peers into the mysteries of the unseen, his foot is planted on the solid ground of external fact; that, in short, the incidents are not invented as a framework for the doctrine, but that the doctrine arises naturally out of, and derives its meaning from, the incidents.

One example will serve at once to illustrate the double characteristic of this Gospel, the accurate historical narrative of facts which forms the basis of the Gospel, and the theological teaching which is built as a superstructure upon this foundation, and which the evangelist keeps distinctly and persistently in view in his selection and arrangement of the facts, and also to introduce the investigation which I purpose instituting.

The narrative and the discourses alike are thoroughly saturated with the Messianic ideas of the time. The Christ, as expected by the Jews, is the one central figure round which all the facts are grouped, the one main topic on which all the conversations hinge. This is the more remarkable because the leading conception in the writer's own mind is not the Messiah, but the Word, the Logos,—not the deliverance of Israel, but the manifestation of God in the flesh. This main purpose is flung out at the opening of the Gospel, and it is kept steadily in view in the selection of materials throughout the work. But it does not once enter into the mind of the Jews, who are wholly absorbed in the Messianic idea. Nay, the word "Logos" does not once occur even on our Lord's own lips, though the obvious motive of his teaching is to enforce this higher aspect of his person, to which they were strangers. And I cannot but think that this distinct separation is a remarkable testimony to the credibility of the writer, who, however strongly impressed with his mission as the teacher of a great theological conception, nevertheless keeps it free from his narrative of facts, though obviously there would be a very strong temptation to introduce it,—a temptation which to a mere forger would be irresistible.

The Messianic idea, for instance, is turned about on all sides, and presented in every aspect. On this point we learn very much more of contemporary Jewish opinion from the Fourth Gospel than from the other three. At the commencement and at the close of the narrative—in the preaching of the Baptist and in the incidents of the passion—it is equally prominent. In Galilee (i. 41, 46, 49, vi. 15, 28, 30 *sq.*), in Samaria (iv. 25, 29, 42), in Judæa (v. 39, 45 *sq.*, vii. 26 *sq.*, 40–43, viii. 30 *sq.*, x. 24), it is the one standard theme of conversation. Among friends, among foes, among neutrals alike, it is mooted and discussed. The person and character of Jesus are tried by this standard. He is accepted or he is rejected as he fulfils or contradicts the received ideal of the Messiah.

The accessories also of the Messiah's coming, as conceived by the Jews, are brought out with a completeness beyond the other Gospels. I will only ask you, as an illustration of this, to consider the discourse on the manna in the sixth chapter. The key to the meaning of the conversation is the fact that the Jews expected a miracle similar to the gift of manna in the wilderness, as an accompaniment of the appearance of the great Deliverer. This expectation throws a flood of light on the whole discourse. But the fact is not communicated in the passage itself. There is only a bald, isolated statement, which apparently is suggested by nothing, and itself fails to suggest anything: "Our fathers did eat manna in the wilderness." Then comes an aposiopesis. The inference is unexpressed. The expectation, which explains all, is left to be inferred, because it would be mentally supplied by men brought up among the ideas of the time. We ourselves have to get it by the aid of criticism and research from rabbinical authorities. But, when we have grasped it, we can unlock the meaning of the whole chapter.

Connected with the Messiah's coming are other conceptions on which it may be worth while to dwell for a moment.

One of these is the appearance of a mysterious person called "*the* prophet." This expectation arose out of the announcement in Deut. xviii. 15, "The Lord thy God will raise up unto thee a prophet from the midst of thee, like unto me." To this anticipation we have allusions in not less than four places in Saint John (i. 21, 25, vi. 14, vii. 40), in all of which "*the* prophet" is mentioned, though in the first three the distinctness of the expectation is blurred in the English version by the rendering "*that* prophet." In all these passages, the mention of "*the* prophet" without any explanation is most natural on the lips of contemporary Jews, whose minds were filled with the Messianic conceptions of the times; while such language is extremely unlikely to have been invented for them more than a century after the date of the supposed occurrences. But the point especially to be observed is that the form which the conception takes is strictly Jewish, and not Christian. Christian teachers identified the prophet foretold by Moses with our Lord himself, and therefore with the Christ. This application of the prophecy is made directly in Saint Peter's speech (Acts iii. 22), and inferentially in Saint Stephen's (Acts vii. 37); and later Christian teachers followed in their steps. But these Jews in Saint John's Gospel conceive of "*the* Christ" and "*the* prophet" as two different persons. If he is not "the Christ," they adopt the alternative that he may be "*the* prophet" (i. 21, 25); if not the prophet, then the Christ (vii. 40). It is hardly conceivable to my mind that a Christian writer living in or after the middle of the second century, calling on his imagination for facts, should have divested himself so absolutely of the Christian idea and fallen back on the Jewish.

But before I have done with "*the* prophet" there is yet one more point worthy of notice. After the miracle of feeding the five thousand, we are told that "those men who had seen the miracle that Jesus did said, This is of a truth *the* prophet that should come into the world" (vi. 14). The connection is not obvious, and the writer has not explained himself. Here, again, the missing link is supplied by the Messianic conception of the age. The prophet foretold was to be like Moses himself. Hence it was inferred that there must be a parallel in the works of the two. Hence a repetition of the gift of the manna — the bread from heaven — might be expected. Was not this miracle, then, the very fulfilment of their expectation? Hence we read that on the day following (after several incidents have intervened, but with the miracle still fresh on their minds) they seek him out, and still try to elicit a definite answer from him: "What sign showest thou, then? Our fathers did eat manna in the desert." Thus a casual and indistinct reference in one part of the chapter is explained by an equally casual and indistinct reference in another, and light emerges from darkness.

From the Messianic ideas I turn to the Jewish sects and the Levitical hierarchy.

The Sadducees, with whom we are familiar in the other Gospels, are not once mentioned by the Fourth Evangelist. How are we to account for this fact? Have we here a discrepancy, or (if not a discrepancy) at least an incongruity? Is there in Saint John's picture an entire omission of that group which occupies a prominent place on the canvas of the other evangelists, especially of Saint Matthew?

The common connection, when describing the adversaries of our Lord, is "the Pharisees and Sadducees" in the synoptic evangelists, "the chief priests and the Pharisees" in Saint John. In the comparison of these phrases lies the solution. The high priests at this time belonged to the sect of the Sadducees. How this happened we do not know. It may be that their Roman rulers favored this party, as being more lukewarm than the Pharisees in religious matters, and therefore less likely to give trouble to the civil powers. At all events, the fact appears distinctly from more than one notice in the narrative of the Acts (iv. 1, v. 17); and the same is stated in a passage of Josephus (*Ant.* xx. 9. 1). Thus a real coincidence arises from an apparent incongruity.

But Josephus elsewhere (*Ant.* xviii. 1. 4) makes another statement respecting the Pharisees, which throws great light on the narrative of the Fourth Evangelist. He tells us that the Sadducees were few in number, though of the highest rank, and that, when they were in office, they were forced, even against their will, to listen to the Pharisees, because otherwise they would not be tolerated by the people. Now, this is precisely the order of events in Saint John. The Pharisees (with one single exception) always take the initiative. They are the active opponents of our Lord, and the chief priests step in to execute their will.

The single exception is remarkable. Once only we find chief priests acting alone and acting promptly (xii. 10). They form a plot of putting Lazarus to death. This was essentially a Sadducees' question. It was necessary that a living witness to the great truth, which the high-priestly party denied, should be got rid of at all hazards. Hence they bestir themselves and throw off their usual apathy, just as, turning from the Gospels to the Acts of the Apostles, they have taken the place of the Pharisees as the foremost persecutors of the new faith, because the resurrection from the dead was the cardinal topic of the preaching of the apostles.

But there is one other notice of the Jewish historian with which the narrative of the Fourth Evangelist presents a striking but unsuspicious coincidence. We are somewhat startled with the outburst of rudeness which marks the chief of the party on one occasion (xi. 49). "One of them, Caiaphas, being high priest that year, said unto them, Ye know nothing at all; and ye do not reflect that it is expedient for you that one man should die for the people, and that the whole nation should not perish." As a comment on this, take the words of Josephus: "The behavior of the Sadducees to one another is not a little rude; and their intercourse with their peers is brusque, as if addressing strangers" (*B. J.* ii. 8. 14).

These coincidences need little comment. I will only add that the Fourth Evangelist does not himself give us the key to the incidents, that the references have been gathered from three different parts of Josephus, that the statements in the evangelist are not embroideries on his narrative, but are woven into its very texture, and that, nevertheless, all these several notices dovetail together and create one harmonious whole, which bears the very impress of strict historical truth.

After reviewing these coincidences, it will appear strange that from the passage last quoted Baur derived what he obviously considered to be one of the strongest arguments against the authenticity of the Gospel. Because the evangelist three times speaks of Caiaphas as "high priest that year" (xi. 49, 51, xviii. 13), he argues that the writer supposed the high priesthood to be an annual office, and therefore could not have been the Apostle John.

Now, unless I have entirely misled you and myself, this is incredible. You cannot imagine that one who shows an acquaintance, not only with the language, but also with the customs, feelings, history, topography, of the race, even in their minute details, should yet be ignorant of this most elementary fact of Jewish institutions. Whether the Gospel is authentic or whether it is not, such a supposition is equally incredible. If the writing is a forgery, the forger was certainly highly informed and extremely subtle. He must have ransacked divers histories for his facts; and yet here he is credited with a degree of ignorance which a casual glance at a few pages of his Old Testament or his Josephus would at once have served to dissipate. Suppose a parallel case. Imagine one who, writing (we will say) a historical work, shows a subtle appreciation of political feeling in England, and a minute acquaintance with English social institutions, and yet falls into the error of supposing that the premier is elected annually by vote of the people, or that the lord-mayoralty is a hereditary office tenable for life. If, therefore, this supposition is simply impossible, we must explain the expression, "high priest that year," in some other way. And the explanation seems to be this. The most important duty of the high priest was an annual function, the sacrifice and intercession for the people on the great day of atonement. "Once every year," says the writer of the Epistle to the Hebrews (ix. 7), "the high priest alone entereth into the second tabernacle [the inner sanctuary], not without blood, which he offereth for himself and for the errors of the people." The year of which the evangelist speaks was the year of all years, the acceptable year of the Lord, as it is elsewhere called, the year in which the great sacrifice, the one atonement, was made, the atonement which annulled once and forever the annual repetitions. It so happened that it was the duty of Caiaphas, as high priest, to enter the holy of holies, and offer the atonement for *that* year. The evangelist sees, if we may use the phrase without irreverence, a dramatic propriety in the fact that he of all men should make this declaration. By a divine irony he is made unconsciously to declare the truth, proclaiming Jesus to be the great atoning sacrifice, and himself to be instrumental in offering the victim. This irony of circumstances is illustrated in the case of Pilate, as in the case of Caiaphas. The latter, the representative of the Jewish hierarchy, pronounces Jesus the great atoning sacrifice; the former, the representative of the civil power, pronounces him as the sovereign of the race, "Behold your King." The malignity of Caiaphas and the sneer of Pilate alike bear witness to a higher truth than they themselves consciously apprehend.

From the sects and the hierarchy we may turn to the city and the temple. Here, too, we should do well to bear in mind how largely we owe the distinctive features of the topography and architecture with which we are familiar to the Fourth Gospel. Within the sacred precincts themselves the Porch of Solomon, within the Holy City the pools of Bethesda and Siloam, are brought before our eyes by this evangelist alone. And when we pass outside of the walls, he is still our guide. From him we trace the steps of the Lord and His disciples on that fatal night crossing the brook Kedron into the garden; it is he who, relating the last triumphal entry into Jerusalem, specifies "*the* branches of the palm-trees" (the other evangelists use general expressions, "boughs of the trees," or the like),—

"*the* palm-trees" on which he had so often gazed, of which the sight was still so fresh in his memory, which clothed the eastern slopes of Olivet, and gave its name to the village of Bethany, "the house of dates." How simple and natural the definite articles are on the lips of an eye-witness I need not say. How awkward they sound to later ears, and how little likely to have been used by a later writer, unfamiliar with its scene itself, we may infer from the fact that in our own version they are suppressed, and the evangelist is made to say, "they took branches of palm-trees."

Moreover, the familiarity of the Fourth Evangelist, not only with the site and the buildings of the temple, but also with the history, appears in a striking way from a casual allusion. After the description of the cleansing of the temple by our Lord,—a description which, though brief, is given with singular vividness of detail,—the Jews ask for some sign as the credential which might justify this assumption of authority and right of chastisement His answer is, "Pull down this temple, and in three days I will build it up." Their astonishment is expressed in their reply, "This temple has been forty-six years in building, and wilt Thou raise it again in three days?" (ii. 19, 20.)

Now I think it will be allowed that this mention of time is quite undesigned. It has no appearance of artifice, it occurs naturally in the course of conversation, and it is altogether free from suspicion, as having been introduced to give a historical coloring to a work of fiction. If so, let us examine its historical bearing.

For this purpose it is necessary to follow two distinct lines of chronological research. We have to investigate the history of the building of the Herodian temple, and we have to ascertain the dates of our Lord's life.

Now, by comparison of several passages in Josephus, and by the exercise of historical criticism upon them, we arrive at the conclusion that Herod commenced his temple about A.U.C. 735; *i.e.*, B.C. 18. It took many years in building, and was not finally completed until A.U.C. 817; *i.e.*, A.D. 64. Thus the works were going on during the whole of the period comprised in the New Testament history. If we add forty-six years to the date of its commencement (A.U.C. 735), we are brought down to A.U.C. 781 or 782; *i.e.*, A.D. 28 or 29.

The chronology of Herod's temple involves one considerable effort of historical criticism. The chronology of our Lord's life requires another. Into this question, however, I need not enter in detail. It is sufficient to remind you that the common date of the Christian era is now generally allowed to be a little wide of the mark, and that our Lord's birth actually took place three or four years before this era. The point to be observed here is that Saint Luke places the baptism of our Lord in or about the fifteenth year of Tiberius, which comprised the interval between the autumn of 781 and the autumn of 782. Now the occurrence related by Saint John took place, as we may infer from his narrative, in the first passover after the baptism; that is, according to Saint Luke's chronology, probably at the passover of 782.

Thus we are brought to the same date by following two lines of chronology; and we arrive at the fact that forty-six years or thereabout had actually elapsed since the commencement of Herod's building to this point in our Lord's ministry. I am anxious not to speak with too great precision, because the facts do not allow it. The exact number might have been forty-five or forty-seven years, for fragments of years may be reckoned in or not in our calculation, and the data are not sufficiently exact to determine the date to a nicety. But, after all allowance made for this margin of uncertainty, the coincidence is sufficiently striking.

And now let us suppose the Gospel to have been written in the middle of the second century, and ask ourselves what strong improbabilities this hypothesis involves.

The writer must first have made himself acquainted with a number of facts connected with the temple of Herod. He must not only have known that the temple was commenced in a particular year, but also that it was still incomplete at the time of our Lord's ministry. So far as we know, he could only have got these facts from Josephus. Even Josephus, however, does not state the actual date of the commencement of the temple. It requires some patient research to arrive at this date by a comparison of several passages. We have therefore to suppose, first, that the forger of the Fourth Gospel went through an elaborate critical investigation for the sake of ascertaining the date. But, secondly, he must have made himself acquainted with the chronology of the gospel history. At all events, he must have ascertained the date of the commencement of our Lord's ministry. The most favorable supposition is that he had before him the Gospel of Saint Luke, though he nowhere else betrays the slightest acquaintance with this Gospel. Here he would find the date which he wanted, reckoned by the years of the Roman emperors. Thirdly, after arriving at these two results by separate processes, he must combine them, thus connecting the chronology of the Jewish kings with the chronology of the Roman emperors, the chronology of the temple erection with the chronology of our Lord's life.

When he has taken all these pains, and worked up the subject so elaborately, he drops in the notice which has given him so much trouble in an incidental and unobtrusive way. It has no direct bearing on his history; it does not subserve the purpose of his theology. It leads to nothing, proves nothing. Certainly, the art of concealing art was never exercised in a more masterly way than here. And yet this was an age which perpetrated the most crude and bungling forgeries, and is denounced by modern criticism for its utter incapacity of criticism.

Nor, when we travel beyond the city and its suburbs, does the writer's knowledge desert him. One instance must suffice; but it is, if I mistake not, so convincing that it may well serve in place of many.

The country of the Samaritans lay between Judæa and Galilee, so that a person journeying from the one region to the other, unless he were prepared to make a détour, must necessarily pass through it. This was the case with our Lord and his apostles, as related in the fourth chapter. The high-road from Jerusalem passes through some very remarkable scenery. The mountain ridges of Ebal and Gerizim run parallel to each other from east to west, not many hundred feet apart, thus enclosing a narrow valley between them. Eastward this little valley opens out into a plain, a rare phenomenon in this country,— "one mass of corn unbroken by a boundary or hedge," as it is described by one who has seen it. Up the valley westward, shut in between these mountain barriers, lies the modern town of Nablûs, the ancient Shechem. The road does not enter the valley, but traverses the plain, running at right angles to the gorge, and thus touching the eastern bases of the mountain ridges as they fall down into the level ground. Here at the mouth of the valley is a deep well, even now descending "to a depth of seventy feet or more," and formerly, before it had been partially filled with accumulated rubbish, we may well believe deeper still. In the words of Dean Stanley: —

> Of all the *special* localities of our Lord's life in Palestine, this is almost the only one absolutely undisputed. By the edge of this well, in the touching language of the ancient hymn, "quærens me sedisti lassus." Here on the great road through which "He must needs go" when "He left Judæa, and departed into Galilee," He halted, as travellers still halt, in the noon or evening of the spring day, by the side of the well. Up that passage through the valley His disciples "went away into the city," which He did not enter. Down the same gorge came the woman to draw water, according to the unchanged custom of the East. . . . Above them, as they talked, rose "this mountain" of Gerizim, crowned by the temple, of which vestiges still remain, where the fathers of the Samaritan sect "said men ought to worship." . . . And round about them, as He and she thus sate or stood by the well, spread far and wide the noble plain of waving corn. It was still winter, or early spring, "four months yet to the harvest," and the bright golden ears of those fields had not yet "whitened" their unbroken expanse of verdure. But, as He gazed upon them, they served to suggest the glorious vision of the distant harvest of the Gentile world, which with each successive turn of the conversation unfolded itself more and more distinctly before Him, as He sate (so we gather from the narrative) absorbed in the opening prospect, silent amidst His silent and astonished disciples.

The scrupulous accuracy of the geographical and archæological details in Saint John's account of the conversation with the Samaritan woman will have appeared already from this quotation. I will only ask you to consider for a moment how naturally they occur in the course of the narrative, so naturally and so incidentally that without the researches of modern travellers the allusions would be entirely lost to us. I think that this consideration will leave but one alternative. Either you have here written, as we are constantly reminded, in an uncritical age and among an uncritical people, the most masterly piece of romance-writing which the genius and learning of man ever penned in any age, or you have (what universal tradition represents it to be) a genuine work of an eye-witness and companion of our Lord. Which of these two suppositions does less violence to historical probability I will leave to yourselves to determine.

Follow then the narrative in detail. An unknown Traveller is sitting at the well. His garb, or His features, or His destination shows him to be a Jew. A woman of the country comes to draw water from the well, and He asks her to give Him to drink. She is surprised that He, a Jew, is willing to talk so freely to her, a Samaritan. And here I would remark that the explanation which follows, "For the Jews have no dealings with" (or, rather, "do not associate with") "the Samaritans," is the evangelist's own, a fact obscured by the ordinary mode of printing in our English Bibles. Hitherto, though the scene is very natural and very real, there is nothing which a fairly clever artist might not have invented. But from this point onwards follow in rapid succession various historical and geographical allusions, various hints of individual character in the woman, various aspects of divine teaching on our Lord's part, all closely interwoven together, each suggesting and suggested by another, in such a manner as to preclude any hypothesis of romance or forgery. "Thou wouldest have asked, and I would have given thee living water." "Sir, Thou hast nothing to draw with, and the well is *deep*. . . . Art Thou greater than our father Jacob?" And so the conversation proceeds, one point suggesting the next in the most natural way. Take, for instance, the reference to Gerizim. "Sir, I perceive that Thou art a prophet. Our fathers worshipped in this mountain." Observe that there is no mention in the context of any mountain in the neighborhood; and even here, where it is mentioned, its name is not given. But suddenly the woman, partly to divert the inconvenient tenor of the conversation, partly to satisfy herself on one important point of difference between the Samaritans and the Jews, avails herself of the newly found prophet's presence, and, pointing to the overhanging heights of Gerizim, puts the question to Him. The mention of the sacred mountain, like the mention of the depth of the well, draws forth a new spiritual lesson. "Not in this mountain, nor yet at Jerusalem. . . . God is a spirit." The woman saith, "When Messias cometh, He will tell us all things." Jesus saith, "I that speak unto thee am He."

At this point the disciples approach from the valley, with the provisions which they had purchased in the city, and rejoin their Master. They are surprised to find Him so engaged. Here, again, an error in the English version obscures the sense. Their marvel was, not that He talked with *the* woman, but that he talked with *a* woman. It was a rabbinical maxim, "Let no man talk with a woman in the street [in public], no, not with his own wife." The narrowness of His disciples was shocked that He, their own rabbi, should be so wanting to Himself as to disregard this recognized precept of morality. The narrator assumes the knowledge with which he himself was so familiar.

So the conversation with the woman closes. With natural eagerness she leaves her pitcher, and hurries back to the city with her news. With natural exaggeration she reports there that the stranger has told her all things that ever she did.

A conversation with the disciples follows, which is hardly less remarkable, but from which I must be content to select one illustration only. I think that it must be allowed that the reference to the harvest is wholly free from suspicion as regards the manner of its introduction. It is unpremeditated; for it cannot be severed from the previous part of the conversation, out of which it arises. It is unobtrusive; for the passage itself makes no attempt to explain the local allusion (which, without the experience of modern travellers, would escape notice): "There are yet four months, and then cometh the harvest. Behold, I say unto you, Lift up your eyes, and look on the fields; for they are white already to harvest." And yet, when we once realize the scene, when in imagination our eye ranges over that vast expanse of growing corn — so unusual in Palestine, however familiar in corn-growing England — we are at once struck with the truthfulness and the significance of this allusive parable.

I have thus endeavored to show, by taking a few instances, the accuracy of the writer's knowledge in all that relates to the history, the geography, the institutions, the thoughts and feelings of the Jews. If, however, we had found accuracy, and nothing more, we might indeed have reasonably inferred that the narrative was written by a Jew of the mother-country, who lived at a very early age, before time and circumstances had obliterated the traces of Palestine, as it existed in the first century; but we could not safely have gone beyond this. But, unless I have entirely deceived myself, the manner in which this accurate knowledge betrays itself justifies the further conclusion that we have before us the genuine narrative of an eye-witness, who records the events just as they occurred in natural sequence.

I have discussed the accuracy of the external allusions. Let me now apply another test. The representation of character is perhaps the most satisfactory criterion of a true narrative, as applied to an age before romance-writing had been studied as an art.

We are all familiar with the principal characters in the gospel history,— Peter, John, Philip, Thomas, Pilate, the sisters Mary and Martha, and several others whom I might mention, each standing before us with an individuality which seems to place him or her within the range of our own personal knowledge. Have we ever asked ourselves to which evangelist above the rest we owe this personal acquaintance with the actors in this great drama?

When the question is once asked, the answer cannot be doubtful. It is true, indeed, that we should have known Saint Peter without the narrative of the Fourth Evangelist, though he adds several minute points, which give additional life to the portrait. It is true that Pilate is introduced to us in the other Gospels, though without Saint John we should not have been able to read his heart and character, his proud Roman indifference and his cynical scorn. But, on the other hand, take the case of Thomas. Of this apostle nothing is recorded in the other evangelists, and yet he stands out before us, not as a mere lay figure, on whose stiff, mechanical form the artist may hang a moral precept or a doctrinal lesson by way of drapery, but as a real, living, speaking man, at once doubtful and eager, at once hesitating and devoted,—sceptical, not because his nature is cold and unsympathetic, but because his intellect moves more cautiously than his heart, because the momentous issues which belief involves bid him pause before he closes with it; at one moment endeavoring to divert his Master's purpose of going up to Jerusalem, where certain destruction awaits Him, at the next ready to share the perils with Him, "Let us also go with Him"; at one moment resisting the testimony of direct eye-witnesses and faithful friends to his Master's resurrection, at the next overwhelmed by the evidence of his senses, and expressing the depth of his conviction in the earnest confession, "my Lord and my God."

I must satisfy myself with one other example. The characters of the sisters Martha and Mary present a striking contrast. They are mentioned once only in the other Gospels, in the familiar passage of Saint Luke, where they appear respectively as the practical, bustling housewife, who is busied about many things, and the devout, contemplative, absorbed disciple, who chooses the one thing needful. In Saint John also this contrast reappears; but the characteristics of the two sisters are brought out in a very subtle way. In Saint Luke the contrast is summed up, as it were, in one definite incident; in Saint John it is developed gradually in the course of a continuous narrative. And there is also another difference. In Saint Luke the contrast is direct and trenchant, a contrast (one might almost say) of light and darkness. But in Saint John the characters are shaded off, as it were, into each other. Both alike are beloved by our Lord, both alike send to Him for help, both alike express their faith in His power, both alike show deep sorrow for their lost brother. And yet notwithstanding this the difference of character is perceptible throughout the narrative. It is Martha who, with her restless activity, goes out to meet Jesus, while Mary remains in the house weeping. It is Martha who holds a conversation with Jesus, argues with Him, remonstrates with Him, and in the very crisis of their grief shows her practical common sense in deprecating the removal of the stone. It is Mary who goes forth silently to meet Him, silently and tearfully, so that the bystanders suppose her to be going to weep at her brother's tomb; who, when she sees Jesus, falls down at His feet; who, uttering the same words of faith in His power as Martha, does not qualify them with the reservation; who infects all the bystanders with the intensity of her sorrow, and crushes the human spirit of our Lord Himself with sympathetic grief.

And, when we turn to the second occasion in which the two sisters are introduced by Saint John, the contrast is still the same. Martha is busied in the homely duties of hospitality towards Jesus and her other guests; but Mary brings her choicest and most precious gift to bestow upon him, at the same time showing the depth of her humility and the abandonment of her devotion by wiping his feet with her hair.

In all this narrative the evangelist does not once direct attention to the contrast between the two sisters. He simply relates the events of which he was an eye-witness without a comment. But the two were real, living persons, and therefore the difference of character between them develops itself in action.

I have shown hitherto that, whatever touchstone we apply, the Fourth Gospel vindicates itself as a trustworthy narrative, which could only have proceeded from a contemporary and an eye-witness. But nothing has hitherto been adduced which leads to the identification of the author as the Apostle Saint John. Though sufficient has been said to vindicate the *authenticity*, the *genuineness* is yet untouched.

It is said by those who deny its apostolic origin that the unknown author, living in the middle of the second century, and wishing to gain a hearing for a modified gospel suited to the wants of his age, dropped his own personality and shielded himself under the name of Saint John the son of Zebedee.

Is this a true representation of the fact? Is it not an entire, though unconscious misrepresentation? John is not once mentioned by name throughout the twenty-one chapters of this Gospel. James and John, the sons of Zebedee, occupy a prominent place in all the other evangelists. In this Fourth Gospel alone neither brother's name occurs. The writer does once, it is true, speak of the "sons of Zebedee"; but in this passage, which occurs in the last chapter (xxi. 2), there is not even the faintest hint of any connection between the writer himself and this pair of brothers. He mentions them in the third person, as he might mention any character whom he had occasion to introduce.

Now, is not this wholly unlike the proceeding of a forger who was simulating a false personality? Would it not be utterly irrational under these circumstances to make no provision for the identification of the author, but to leave everything to the chapter of accidents? No discredit, indeed, is thrown on the genuineness of a document by the fact that the author's name appears on the forefront. This is the case with the histories of Herodotus and Thucydides; it is the case also with the Epistles of Paul and Peter and James, and with the Apocalypse of John. But, on the supposition of forgery, it was a matter of vital moment that the work should be accepted as the genuine production of its pretended author. The two instances of early Christian forgeries which I brought forward in an earlier part of this lecture will suffice as illustrations. The *Gospel of the In-*

fancy closes with a distinct declaration that it was written by James. The *Clementine Homilies* affirm the pretended authorship in the opening words, "I, Clement, being a Roman citizen." Even if our supposed forger could have exercised this unusual self-restraint in suppressing the simulated author's name, would he not have made it clear by some allusion to his brother James, or to his father Zebedee, or to his mother Salome? The policy which he has adopted is as suicidal as it is unexpected.

How, then, do we ascertain that it was written by John, the son of Zebedee? I answer, first of all, that it is traditionally ascribed to him, as the *Phædo* is ascribed to Plato or the *Antigone* to Sophocles; and, secondly, that from a careful examination of indirect allusions and casual notices, from a comparison of things said and things unsaid, we arrive at the same result by a process independent of external tradition. But a forger could not have been satisfied with trusting to either of these. External tradition was quite beyond the reach of his control. In this particular case, as we shall see, the critical investigation requisite is so subtle, and its subject-matter lies so far below the surface, that a forger, even supposing him capable of constructing the narrative, would have defeated his own purpose by making such demands on his readers.

For let us follow out this investigation. In the opening chapter of the Gospel there is mention of a certain disciple whose name is not given (i. 35, 37, 40). This anonymous person (for it is a natural though not a certain inference that the same is meant throughout) reappears again in the closing scene before and after the passion, where he is distinguished as the disciple whom Jesus loved. At length, but not till the concluding verses of the Gospel, we are told that this anonymous disciple is himself the writer: "This is the disciple which testifieth of these things, and wrote these things."

In accordance with this statement, we find that those particular scenes in which this anonymous disciple is recorded as taking a part are related with peculiar minuteness and vividness of detail. Such is the case, for instance, with the notices of the Baptist and of the call of the earliest disciples. Such, again, is the case with the conversation at the last supper, with the scene over the fire in the hall of Caiaphas's house, with certain other incidents connected with the crucifixion, and with the scene on the Lake of Galilee after the resurrection.

Who, then, is this anonymous disciple? On this point the Gospel furnishes no information. We arrive at the identification partly by a process of exhaustion, partly by attention to some casual incidents and expressions.

Comparing the accounts in the other Gospels, it seems safe to assume that he was one of the inner circle of disciples. This inner circle comprised the two pairs of brothers, Peter and Andrew, James and John, if, indeed, Andrew deserves a place here. Now, he cannot have been Andrew, because Andrew appears in company with him in the opening chapter. Nor can he have been Peter, because we find him repeatedly associated with Peter in the closing scenes. Again, James seems to be excluded; for James fell an early martyr, and external and internal evidence alike point to a later date for this Gospel. Thus, by a process of exhaustion, we are brought to identify him with John, the son of Zebedee.

With this identification all the particulars agree.

First. He is called among the earliest disciples; and, from his connection with Andrew (i. 40, 44), it may be inferred that he was a native of Bethsaida in the neighborhood.

Secondly. At the close of his Master's life, and after his Master's resurrection, we find him especially associated with Simon Peter. This position exactly suits John, who in the earliest days of the Church takes his place by the side of Peter in the championship of faith.

Thirdly. Unless the beloved disciple be John, the son of Zebedee, this person who occupies so prominent a place in the account of the other evangelists, and who stood in the foremost rank in the estimation of the early Church as a pillar apostle, does not once appear in the Fourth Gospel, except in the one passage where "the sons of Zebedee" are mentioned and summarily dismissed in a mere enumeration of names. Such a result is hardly credible.

Lastly. Whereas in the other evangelists John the Baptist is very frequently distinguished by the addition of this surname, and always so distinguished where there is any possibility of confusing him with the son of Zebedee, in this Gospel alone the forerunner is never once called John the Baptist. To others some distinguishing epithet seemed needed. To the son of Zebedee there was only one famous John; and, therefore, when he had occasion to mention him, he naturally spoke of him as John simply, without any addition. Is it conceivable, I would ask, that any forger would have lost sight of himself so completely, and used the natural language of John, the son of Zebedee, with such success as to observe this very minute and unobtrusive indication of personality?

I have addressed myself more directly to the theory of the Tübingen school, either as propounded by Baur or as modified by later critics, which denies at once the historical character of this Gospel and its apostolic authorship, and places it in the middle or the latter half of the second century. But there is an intermediate position between rejecting its worth as a historic record and accepting Saint John as its author, and this position has been taken up by some. They suppose it to have been composed by some disciple or disciples of Saint John from reminiscences of their master's teaching, and thus they are prepared to allow that it contains some historical matter which is valuable. You will have seen, however, that most of the arguments adduced, though not all, are equally fatal to this hypothesis as the other. The process by which, after establishing its authenticity, we succeeded in identifying its author, is, if I mistake not, alone sufficient to overthrow this solution. Indeed, this theory is exposed to a double set of objections, and it has nothing to recommend it.

I have already taken up more time than I had intended, and yet I feel that very much has been left unsaid. But I venture to hope that certain lines of investigation have been indicated, which, if carefully and soberly followed out, can only lead to one result. Whatever consequences may follow from it, we are compelled on critical grounds to accept this Fourth Gospel as the genuine work of John, the son of Zebedee.

Some among my hearers perhaps may be disappointed that I have not touched on some well-known difficulties, though these have been grossly exaggerated. Some have been satisfactorily explained; of others probable, or at least possible, solutions have been given; while others still remain on which we are obliged to suspend judgment until some new light of history is vouchsafed. It is not from too much light, but from too little light, that the historical credibility of this Gospel has suffered. Each new discovery made, each old fact elucidated, sets at rest some disputed question. If the main fact of the genuineness be established, the special difficulties can well afford to wait.

One word more, and I conclude. I have treated this as a purely critical question, carefully eschewing any appeal to Christian instincts. As a critical question, I wish to take a verdict upon it. But, as I could not have you think that I am blind to the theological issues directly or indirectly connected with it, I will close with this brief confession of faith. I believe from my heart that the truth which this Gospel more especially enshrines — the truth that Jesus Christ is the very Word incarnate, the manifestation of the Father to mankind — is the one lesson which, duly apprehended, will do more than all our feeble efforts to purify and elevate human life here by imparting to it hope and light and strength,— the one study which alone can fitly prepare us for a joyful immortality hereafter.

www.ingramcontent.com/pod-product-compliance
Lightning Source LLC
Chambersburg PA
CBHW030847270326
41928CB00007B/1252
9783337281496